Perfect Best Man

George Davidson is a former senior editor with Chambers Harrap. He is an experienced researcher and writer of reference books and has participated in several weddings as bridegroom, best man, and father of the bride. He lives in Edinburgh.

Other titles in the *Perfect* series

Perfect Answers to Interview Questions – Max Eggert
Perfect Babies' Names – Rosalind Fergusson
Perfect CV – Max Eggert
Perfect Interview – Max Eggert
Perfect Numeracy Test Results – Joanna Moutafi and Ian Newcombe
Perfect Personality Profiles – Helen Baron
Perfect Psychometric Test Results – Joanna Moutafi and Ian Newcombe
Perfect Pub Quiz – David Pickering
Perfect Punctuation – Stephen Curtis
Perfect Readings for Weddings – Jonathan Law
Perfect Wedding Speeches and Toasts – George Davidson

Perfect
Best Man

George Davidson

BOOKS

Published by Random House Books 2007

2 4 6 8 10 9 7 5 3 1

First published in the United Kingdom in 2007 by
Random House Books

Random House Books
Random House, 20 Vauxhall Bridge Road,
London SW1V 2SA

www.randomhouse.co.uk

Addresses for companies within The Random House Group Limited
can be found at: www.randomhouse.co.uk/offices.htm

The Random House Group Limited Reg. No. 954009

A CIP catalogue record for this book
is available from the British Library

ISBN 9781905211784

The Random House Group Limited makes every effort to ensure that the
papers used in its books are made from trees that have been legally sourced
from well-managed and credibly certified forests. Our paper procurement
policy can be found at: www.randomhouse.co.uk/paper.htm

Typeset by Palimpsest Book Production Limited, Grangemouth, Stirlingshire

Printed in the UK by CPI Bookmarque, Croydon, CR0 4TD

Contents

The author would like to thank Sophie Lazar, Emily Rhodes, and Gareth Blatchford for their helpful comments on earlier drafts of this book, and the Rev. John Davidson for his useful suggestions and advice.

Introduction

If you are looking at this book, you are probably in one of two situations:

- You have been asked to be the best man at a wedding, but before making up your mind about whether to say 'yes' or 'no', you want to know more about what is involved; or
- You have already agreed to be someone's best man, but are now beginning to wonder what you have let yourself in for.

Whichever position you are in, this book can help you. It will take you step by step through the whole business of being a best man, from the moment you agree to take on the job, which is when your responsibilities begin, to the day after the wedding, when your responsibilities will be over. If you follow the guidance provided in this book, you will know:

- what you have to do
- how you should do it
- what problems might arise
- how to handle them if they do.

And that is all you need to know to be the perfect best man.

So *relax*. **There is nothing about being a best man that you can't handle.** You've got plenty of time. Take the wedding preparations and organisation bit by bit, follow this book's instructions and advice, and everything will be fine.

What is in this book?

In chapters one to three, you will find a brief overview of **what is involved in being a best man**, a description of the **main qualities and skills a best man should have** (and how to acquire them if you don't already have them), and a discussion of **reasons you might have for turning down an invitation to be a best man.**

After that, the book takes you chapter by chapter through every stage of the **wedding preparations, the wedding ceremony, and the wedding reception**, from meeting the families and organising the stag party, through what to wear on the day, and on to how to write and deliver the best man's speech.

Everything *should* be under control, but what if . . . ? With this in mind, there are in many chapters **troubleshooting panels** that give you guidance on how to plan for and deal with problems that *might* arise. If something *does* go wrong at a wedding, it is usually not the best man's fault, but if you have worked out in advance what to do if any of these things do happen, you will be better able to handle the situation calmly.

At the end of the book you will find a **Quick Quotes** section providing some material for your best man's speech, and four **Quick Reference** sections, covering: the duties of the best man and the ushers; a step-by-step wedding timetable of what to do as preparations progress; a set of useful *checklists*; and further sources of advice and information.

Nothing is left to chance, and nothing is left for you to think out or guess at for yourself. Everything you need is here.

The female 'best man'

Throughout this book, it is assumed that the best man is male. This need not, however, be the case. It is not unknown nowadays for a female friend or relative to be invited to be the 'best man' (the 'best woman', or simply the 'bridegroom's attendant') at a wedding. While for simplicity of style, the best man is always referred to in this book as 'he', almost everything that is said that applies to a male best man would apply equally well to a female best man. The only differences would be in what she should wear (and appropriate dress for a female best man is discussed in chapter six), and whether she should organise the stag party (see chapter nine).

Best men?

It is becoming increasingly common for there to be more than one best man, and there is nothing in marriage law or marriage etiquette to disallow it. In which case, it is up to the two (or more!) best men to discuss their roles with the groom and come to an agreement about who is to be responsible for what. (After all, only one best man can actually carry the ring – unless there are two rings – but the other best man could be one of the witnesses at the ceremony; and while probably only one best man should make a speech, the other one could act as master of ceremonies at the reception or read out the letters and cards from well-wishers. But see page 109 for alternative suggestions.)

Check with the church, etc.

Although there is nothing to disallow a female best man or two best men, it would be wise of the groom to check with the person who will be performing the marriage ceremony that they have no objection to this. You do not want it to be a subject of disagreement or disapproval (or a downright ban) either at the wedding rehearsal two or three days before the wedding, or on the day itself.

The perfect best man

Does the perfect best man actually exist? Perhaps; perhaps not. But if you follow the advice in this book, you will come so close to perfection that no one will notice or care about any minor imperfections.

Perfect Best Man tells you all you need to know about your duties and how to carry them out **efficiently** and **effectively** and, no less important, **enjoyably**.

1 Outline of the best man's duties

In a nutshell, the best man's principal duty is **to help and advise the bridegroom during the period of preparation for the wedding and through the wedding day itself.** He is the groom's right-hand man, his Man Friday, his trouble-shooter and problem-solver.

But the best man's duty is not solely to the bridegroom: he also owes it to the bride and to both families to see that everything runs smoothly before as well as on the day.

Have you ever been involved in a political campaign? A marketing campaign? A military campaign? Well, you could look on a wedding as a sort of 'marriage campaign'.

What is the aim of the campaign? To see two people happily married and safely off on their honeymoon.

And who is the campaign manager? You are. The best man.

A little bit of history

It may seem a bit far-fetched to compare the duties of a best man to a military campaign, but actually, in times past (when it was not uncommon for men to raid castles, towns and villages to carry off their brides by force) the two things were not so very different.

In those days, the 'best man' would be the strongest of the would-be bridegroom's friends or relatives, chosen not for his speech-making or party-organising abilities but for his trustworthiness, prowess, and swordsmanship. His job would be to help fight off the girl's family during the raid and to protect her and the bridegroom until they were safely married, often going so far as accompanying them up the aisle.

It is said that this is also the reason why the best man traditionally stands to the right of the bridegroom during the wedding ceremony: as protector of the bride and groom, he needed to keep his right hand, his sword hand, unobstructed and ready for action.

The best man may be the campaign manager but he does not, of course, have to organise everything himself – a good manager knows *how* to delegate and *what* to delegate (and if *you* don't, this book will tell you). The size of the bride's and groom's families may also affect how much you as best man will have to deal with personally: some jobs may be taken off your hands and given to members of the family. This is something to discuss in the planning meetings you will have with the bride and groom.

The groom, the bride, and others have their own particular tasks to attend to, but as the best man and campaign manager, it will be up to you to see that everything is done as it should be, at the right time, and by the right person.

A wedding day should be a memorable day for all the right reasons, not the wrong ones. No one wants to look back on a wedding catastrophe.

Your job as best man is simply to do everything you can to avoid disaster and ensure success.

And the key to this is . . . **preparation, preparation, preparation.**

The key elements of the marriage campaign

Within the 'marriage campaign' there are **three key events** that particularly involve the best man (though not all marriages will necessarily involve all three):

- the marriage ceremony
- a wedding reception after the ceremony
- a stag party at some point before the ceremony.

The marriage ceremony

Obviously, no matter what else is planned for the wedding, there is going to be a wedding ceremony of some sort held somewhere. Here, you as best man will have **two key duties:**

- Your most important task in the whole marriage campaign will be to get yourself and the groom to the ceremony awake, sober, properly dressed, and on time.
- Your second most important task will be to get the wedding ring from the groom at some point before the ceremony, to keep it safe, and to produce it – without dropping it! – when required during the ceremony.

Succeed in these two tasks and you will be forgiven almost anything else; but fail in these responsibilities . . . well, you probably know the saying about hell having no fury like a woman scorned – and you will have the bride, the bride's mother, and the bridegroom's mother to answer to!

What other responsibilities you may have will depend to a great extent on the style and formality of the ceremony, and whether it is being held in a church or a registry office (or on the couple's favourite beach, or halfway up a mountain). A small, informal registry office wedding will, of course, involve much less organisation than a large, formal church ceremony. (As for getting the wedding party and all the guests up a mountain, let's just not go there now. Though with planning and preparation, it can be done.)

At the end of the wedding ceremony comes the signing of the marriage register. Two witnesses are legally required to sign this document, and you may be asked to be one of them.

Beyond that, you have little to do. If there are ushers at the wedding, as there probably will be at a church ceremony, they will act as your assistants, and it will be up to you to brief them on their duties. What these duties might be is covered in Quick Reference List 1 (page 125) and in chapters eight and thirteen.

The wedding reception

The wedding reception is sometimes known as the 'wedding breakfast' (though it is not normally held at breakfast time!). Again, your duties as best man will vary depending on the formality and size of the event. You may have very little to do at all by way of organisation and responsibilities, beyond one thing – the best man's speech.

The best man's speech at the reception is probably the most dreaded part of the best man's duties, but it needn't be. It doesn't have to be a long speech, though there are certain things you do have to say in the speech (these are explained in chapter fifteen), and it doesn't have to be brilliantly witty (though in the Quick Quotes appendix at the end of the book there are a few pages of amusing quotations and sayings that you could use if you need to).

The speech may not be all you are called upon to do at the reception. Again, depending on the size and formality of the event, you may be asked to announce the guests by name when they come into the reception and go to greet the receiving line (i.e. the bride and groom, and their parents). It is possible that the hotel/restaurant/caterer may provide someone to do this, but if the responsibility is given to you, don't worry: you don't have to know everyone by name – they tell you who they are and then you announce them.

Beyond that, it is your job (and it is useful if you have the assistance of the ushers or some friends you have recruited in advance) to keep things running smoothly by chatting to guests, making introductions, offering drinks around (unless there are serving staff to do this), helping people to their seats, and so on.

If the reception is followed by a party and dancing, it is part of your responsibility as best man to make sure that everyone is having a good time and that no one is left out. There should be no one sitting alone at a table, and no wallflowers. You cannot do this on your own – you should feel free to co-opt your friends and ushers for the task.

The stag party

There may or may not be a stag party – it is not actually obligatory. If there is, it may involve nothing more than you and the groom having a night out with a few friends (a meal, say, or a few drinks in a pub, and perhaps also a theatre show or a film).

On the other hand, stag parties nowadays often involve weekends or longer holidays away with a group of friends to any of the many towns or activity centres in the UK, on the continent, and even further afield, that now particularly cater for stag events. Such stag events away may include any of a wide range of activities, from paintballing to tank-driving to scuba-diving. Whatever is planned for your groom's stag party, chapter nine takes you step by step through the planning and booking process (though the entire responsibility for organising and booking the event need not rest with the best man alone).

Still worried?

Does the responsibility of being a best man still seem daunting? It shouldn't. Remember that although you will be the campaign manager, you will not be working alone.

Through the whole preparation period for the wedding, you (and the bridesmaid or matron of honour*, if there is one) will be discussing and planning the details of the event with the bride and groom and their families. *They* are the ones who have to make most of the decisions (*your* job is to make sure that they do so in good time, helped along by the

---

* A matron of honour is a married bridesmaid. There may of course be two or more bridesmaids (and in this instance there is likely to be a chief bridesmaid), but from here on we will simply talk about 'the bridesmaid' to cover one or more bridesmaids and or matrons of honour.

occasional tactful question or piece of advice). You have to check, and check again, that everything that needs to be done has been done – but you *don't* have to do everything yourself.

All the planning information you will need is provided for you in this book. Follow the guidelines and the timetables and add in or mark off the items on the checklists week by week and, as the wedding day comes nearer, day by day, and you can't go wrong. Everything will be under control, and you will know for certain that it is.

And don't forget that if you do need help, you can call on professionals as well as friends: registrars, ministers and vicars, dress-hire companies, travel agents, caterers – they are all there to help, and have a wealth of experience to call on. You don't have to know *everything* – if in doubt just ask the experts.

2 Have you got what it takes to be a best man?

Are there any special qualities and skills that a best man should have, and do you have them?

It has been said that the ideal best man should combine the best attributes of 'a teacher, consultant, confessor, psychologist, manager, executive director, security guard, bodyguard, orator, diplomat, godfather and marriage guidance counsellor'.

How many of these do you think you've got? And if you don't have them, what can you do about it? Well, let's cut down that list a bit and consider the key qualities and skills that you might need as best man:

- reliability
- organisational ability
- wedding knowledge
- tact
- ability to deal with problems
- punctuality
- being at ease with strangers
- soberness.

We can add to these general qualities two particular skills that you might feel you would need at the reception:

- public-speaking skills
- an ability to dance.

Is panic rising? Are you worried that you have none of these skills, or not enough of them? Should you say 'no' after all? Well, let's keep things in perspective. A best man is not expected to be Superman. And a *good* best man is simply a *well-prepared* best man. With preparation and planning, there is no reason why you should not manage all the best man's responsibilities to everyone's satisfaction. And enjoy yourself to boot.

So let's look at these 'perfect best man' qualities and skills in more detail.

Reliability

Are you someone who can be relied on, or have you let others down in the past? Perhaps you are not good at saying 'no' and take on more jobs than you really have time to attend to properly. Or perhaps you take on jobs and then simply lose interest in them.

Only you can fix this. If you already have as many responsibilities as you can handle, **you have to decide *now* where your priorities will lie over the next few months.**

If you want to be best man, you have to be both determined and able to do all that is required of you. If you have too many other responsibilities that might prevent you from doing this, you have only two choices: drop some of these responsibilities (for the time being) or turn down the invitation to be best man.

And if you do say 'yes' now, don't take on any further responsibilities until the wedding is over.

Organisational skills

As we have said, as best man you are going to be the manager of the marriage campaign. So ask yourself, are you a good organiser?

Perhaps you have run a campaign before, or organised an event of some sort. If so, you already know how well you coped. Some people are born organisers, and some aren't. If you come into the former category, you are already over a major hurdle. But if you know that you aren't a good organiser, or if you don't know whether you are or not, you are going to need some help to see you through.

Don't despair. That is what this book is for. It tells you exactly what needs to be done, and when, and by whom. All you have to do is use the information in the following chapters and the checklists in the Quick Reference section.

Wedding knowledge

Organisational ability is, of course, not enough on its own. As best man, you will also need to be well informed. You may need to give advice, answer questions, and solve problems. You will need to know what must be done, by whom, and by when, throughout the entire wedding preparation period, and on the wedding day itself. And you will need to know the format of the ceremony, and of the reception: that is, where you, the groom, and the other main participants should be, and what they should be doing, at any given time. Other people may forget things; your job will be to remind them.

Here again, this book, with its detailed chapter-by-chapter guidance, will tell you what you need to know, or at least *most* of what you need to know. Obviously, there may be particular details of the wedding you will be involved in that cannot be described here, but you will sort them out during the planning and preparation period, and with the guidance this book provides, you will be sure not to forget to ask all the necessary questions.

Tact and diplomacy

While the best man was once chosen for his ability to fight, now it is more important that the best man should be able to *prevent* fights and other unpleasantness. Throughout the preparation and planning period, disagreements may arise and tempers may get frayed. You and the bridesmaid may have to calm things down. And on the wedding day itself when people will perhaps be a little tense, and towards the end of the day when they might be getting tired, you may need to be a diplomat as well as a trouble-shooter. Are someone's children being noisy and disruptive? Is there someone who has been drinking a little too much? Are there people who are clearly not getting on, to the point of being belligerent?

You may not have to sort out any of these problems on your own – all that may be required of you is to have a quiet word with someone else who can. The key here, as in so many of your duties as best man, is preparation: you should have found out in advance from the groom and the bride where any potential difficulties could arise, and have a plan to deal with them already in mind before the wedding day.

Ability to handle crises calmly

Most weddings pass off successfully, with no serious problems, and only a few, if any, minor hitches. But of course there are any number of things that *could* go wrong, and you as best man will be the one who has to deal with them. So along with tact and diplomacy, a best man should be able to handle problems, even serious crises, quickly, calmly, and efficiently.

Are you confident in a crisis, or do you usually panic and go to pieces? You certainly can't afford to lose your head when you are the best man, because people will be looking to you for leadership and decisive action.

Here again, the key is preparation. Plan ahead – if something did go wrong on the day, what would you do about it? And who could you call on, if necessary, to help you? Read the troubleshooting panels, follow their suggestions as they might apply to 'your' wedding, and you will have no reason to worry about wedding disasters.

Punctuality

Are you the sort of person people might say would be late for your own funeral? Well, this is one day when you just cannot afford to be late for anything. In particular, it's your job to get yourself and the groom to the wedding ceremony on time.

Planning is again the key. Make a timetable for the day (see the wedding timetable in the Quick Reference section), and *keep to it*.

If you are liable to sleep in, then have several very loud alarm clocks set to go off one after the other at two-minute intervals, book a telephone alarm call (call up the operator at your telephone service the day before the wedding), or get someone reliable to come and waken you – whatever it takes to get you up and about on time.

Sociability

How many people you will have to talk to on the day depends on how large the wedding is to be. Perhaps you already know everyone who will be there, and will feel totally at ease with them all. On the other hand, if you are to be best man at a large and formal 'society' wedding, you may be anxious about how to handle the social side of the day, talking to complete strangers without getting tongue-tied or making a fool of yourself.

There is one key thing to remember: you are the best man. The guests will want to talk to you. They will be interested in you. And they will be pleased and flattered if you show that you are interested in talking to them.

Some pre-wedding preparation will help too. Get to know from the bride and groom a little about the guests you don't know, especially close family members. Looking at photographs may help, so that you know who the main guests are before you meet them. Find out where they live, what they do, what their interests are. Once you have a hook to hang a conversation on, chatting to people is easy.

Sobriety

Unless this is a teetotal wedding, it is more than likely that you will have a few drinks before the day is over. There is, of course, nothing wrong with that. But know when to stop. (This is just a matter of common sense.) Don't forget that you have responsibilities throughout the day and evening, and an excessive intake of alcohol will be of no help in getting you through the best man's speech.

Some people recommend that the groom and best man have a quiet drink together before the ceremony, to keep the groom calm. Again there is nothing wrong with that, so long as it is just one drink. It mustn't get out of hand, and it is your job to see that it doesn't.

And of course one mustn't forget the stag night, if there is one. Here again, while you are out to enjoy yourself, you must remember that it is your responsibility to stay sober enough to get the groom home safely.

Oratorial skills

We have mentioned the best man's speech several times now. But does the best man *have* to give a speech? Well, at least by tradition he does. There *may* be no speeches at an informal post-wedding meal, but as best man you will probably be expected to say *something*. And at a more formal reception you will certainly be expected to 'perform'.

Are you willing to stand up and make a speech at the reception? It's not as daunting a task as it might seem, and you needn't be on your feet for very long, but if you feel it really would be beyond you, then other arrangements will have to be made. You *could* be the best man at the ceremony but have someone else – a member of the family or a close friend – make the speech in your place at the reception, but that would be rather unusual.

If you are worrying about making a speech, **remember three things:**

- A good speech is important but **no one is expecting you to be a brilliant, polished, professional after-dinner speaker** (unless, of course, you are!). Don't try too hard to impress the other guests. Just be yourself.
- **Your speech should probably not last more than four or five minutes.** The time will pass very quickly when you are speaking, and you won't need a lot of speech to fill five minutes (and part of the time is in any case taken up with reading out messages

from well-wishers, which is traditionally the final part of the best man's speech).

- **You will be among friends,** so just be relaxed about your speech. Everyone else will be. No one will be out to criticise you, unless you give them something to criticise – so avoid inappropriate remarks and jokes that some people might consider to be in poor taste.

If you are not an experienced and confident speaker, chapter fifteen explains how to write and deliver the best man's speech, and the Quick Quotes will provide you with some material that you could use if you can't think of anything suitable yourself.

Dancing skills

Once upon a time almost everyone could dance. Dancing classes were a part of a young person's life, almost a rite of passage. But not any more.

So perhaps you can't waltz or quickstep, but you know you may have to at the reception. What do you do? It's all down to planning and preparation again.

First of all, find out straightaway what sort of reception is going to be organised. Will there be dancing, and if so, what sort of dancing? Are you going to have to waltz with the bride, the bride's mother, the bridesmaid?

You won't have to win any prizes for your dancing, but you should be able to get round the floor in time to the music and without tripping up, bumping into people, or standing on your partner's feet. So make sure that you can. Set aside time over the next few months to learn the basics, and **practise**. Practise with your girlfriend, practise with your mother, practise with the bridesmaid (who will probably be your partner at some point in the evening). It's worth the effort and it will add to your enjoyment on the night.

3 Should you say 'yes' or 'no'?

Now that you have read chapters one and two, you know roughly what will be expected of you as a best man. So, is it time for you to confirm that you will accept the job? Well, perhaps not *quite* yet. First, you need to stop, think, and answer three important questions:

- Am I willing to accept the responsibilities that being the best man would entail?
- Is there anything that might get in the way of my ability to do the job?
- Is there someone else to whom the invitation should have been extended?

Accepting the best man's responsibilities

The responsibilities associated with the post of best man needn't be thought of as overwhelming (and this book will ensure that you are not overwhelmed by them), but neither should they be taken lightly.

If you agree to be someone's best man, you are making a serious commitment – to them, to their bride-to-be, and to both their families – that you will do everything that is required of you, as conscientiously and efficiently as you can, from the moment you say 'yes' to the moment the last of your tasks is completed (probably on the day after the wedding).

If the groom needs practical help, for example because he will be out of town, or even out of the country, for much of the time before the wedding, you must be someone he can rely on totally to organise things on his behalf.

So if what you are thinking of at the moment is how much you are going to enjoy a stag weekend in Prague or what a great opportunity being best man will afford you of chatting up the bride's sister, then perhaps you are really not taking your coming responsibilities seriously enough.

As best man, your first responsibility will be to other people, not to yourself. It will be your job to ensure that everything goes smoothly on the day, and that everyone else has a day to remember.

Hopefully you *will* enjoy yourself as well (and maybe get to spend some time with the bride's sister too), but that is not the point of being the best man.

So, stop and think. Do you *really* want to do the job, accept all that it entails, and do it to the very best of your ability? If not, say 'no' now, and let the groom find someone else who *will* do the job properly. (And you needn't read any more of this book.)

Perhaps you could offer to help out in some other way, for example by being an usher and so playing a useful organisational role on the wedding day yet avoiding all the best man's responsibilities. But don't worry – whatever you do, I'm sure you'll still be invited to the wedding, and the stag party!

The most important thing is not to feel pressurised into doing something you really do not want to do or feel you couldn't do. Better to say 'no' straightaway than to agree to do it and then spend the next few months in a flat panic. You'll be no help at all to the groom when he most needs your support and assistance.

Is there anything that might get in the way of you doing the job?

You are willing to accept the responsibilities of being best man, and you are satisfied that you have (or can acquire) the qualities and skills required to see you through. Two things you now have to do before saying 'yes' or 'no' is to look at your **diary** and look at your **bank account**.

Your diary

Are you actually going to be *available*, both on the day and during the run-up to it? This may seem an obvious question, but it is surprising how many people do not consider it before agreeing to be a best man.

There is no point in saying 'yes' to being best man if you actually might have to be elsewhere on the day. So think for a moment. Are you sure you can get time off work? Might your job suddenly require you to be out of town? Is yours the sort of job in which you could be called out to an emergency without warning? Have you perhaps got an exam to study for or a dissertation to hand in around that time? Might your wife or partner be due to give birth to your baby close to the big day? (And don't forget that babies can be quite unpredictable in their arrival dates: a theoretical nine months in the womb doesn't mean *exactly* nine months.) Have you an elderly and frail relative who might need you? Is there *anything* you know of that might keep you away on the day or make you unable to carry out any of your other duties?

Of course, the unexpected happens, but it would be irresponsible to say 'yes' now while knowing perfectly well that something might oblige you to withdraw later on. At the very least, you must let the groom know about this something and fully discuss the implications with him.

If the day of the wedding has not yet been set, then clearly none of the above applies . . . yet. Your availability on any particular day proposed for the wedding is something that will have to be taken into account later on. (See chapter five on the planning meetings.)

Your bank account

The other question you need to ask yourself is: 'Can I afford it?'

There aren't a lot of costs attached to being a best man, but you may need a new suit, you may feel you will have to give a more expensive present than you would have had you merely been a guest at the wedding, and there may be travel and accommodation costs involved. And can you afford a stag holiday on the continent, if that is what is going to be organised?

You should not let such financial worries immediately deter you from saying 'yes' – there are ways round most problems, and the groom may offer to pay the travel and accommodation expenses of the best man and the ushers – but as with any diary problems you are aware of, you should again let the groom know at once of any financial worries you have and talk them over with him.

Stepping aside for someone else

What do you do if there is another person who you think would want to be the best man? Perhaps, for example, you are the groom's best friend, but you are pretty sure his brother would expect to be asked.

This is not directly your problem, and the groom must have had his reasons for asking you to be his best man rather than someone else, but for the sake of avoiding ill-feeling, it would be wise to raise the matter with the groom and offer to step aside. If you are to be the best man, you are at least entitled to know that you will not be resented by members of the groom's family for usurping the role.

How to reply to the invitation

If you have been invited to be a best man, how should you reply? Simply by saying 'yes' (or 'no') the next time you meet the groom? Or by telephone? Or is something more formal required?

Perhaps the best principle to adopt is to reply in the same manner as you have been asked. If the groom has simply spoken to you one day and asked you to be his best man, then it would not be impolite to reply in the same way, whether face-to-face or by phone. But if you have been asked by email or more formally in a letter, then it would be polite to reply by email or letter in return.

How to make a tactful refusal

Turning down an invitation to be best man needs to be handled tactfully, but as honestly as possible. If you have decided to say 'no', you should do so as soon as possible, so that the groom can ask someone else. Thank the groom for the offer, explain the reason for your decision, express your regret, and leave it at that.

If you have said 'yes' . . .

If you have said yes to being the best man, what are the first things you should do? There are two important things:

- put the wedding date in your diary
- rearrange your schedule if necessary.

If the date and time of the wedding have been decided, then you will already have checked your diary to see that you are available before saying 'yes'. Now is the time to go back to your diary and, if you haven't done so already, write down 'wedding', as well as the time of the wedding, at the appropriate date.

Plan to have as few outside commitments as possible during the week before the wedding, because you will certainly have some wedding commitments (such as the wedding rehearsal, or a pre-wedding meal with the bride and groom, their families, and the bridesmaid). You may also have to deal with unexpected problems – that is part of your job as best man. You don't necessarily have to take the whole week before the wedding off work, but you would be well advised to be completely free for the entire day before the wedding, and don't forget that you may have some duties to attend to on the day after the wedding as well. So make sure you mark off all these days in your dairy.

If the date of the wedding has not yet been decided, then do impress on the bride and groom the need for a prompt decision, so that you and the bridesmaid, and others who will be involved, know when they will be needed. And since you have now agreed to be the best man, you should be involved in the decision-making, since the date agreed on for the wedding has to suit you as much as anyone else in the wedding party.

If you do have prior commitments for the wedding day, but you are sure that they can be rearranged and are therefore no impediment to your being the best man, now is the time to rearrange your schedule. Don't leave it until the last minute, in case you find that you cannot in fact get out of the commitments you had. At that point, you are going to let someone down badly.

An engagement present?

Is an engagement present necessary? Well, perhaps not absolutely necessary, but it's a nice gesture.

Many people give a newly engaged couple a relatively inexpensive present along with their congratulations, and there is no reason for you to do more than that. It is not the main wedding present, just a small gift of something that you know the couple will appreciate.

4 The engagement party

You already know the groom, of course, and perhaps you know the bride, but you may or may not have met their families, and you may not know the bridesmaid. So if possible, and as soon as possible, you should get to know all the members of the wedding party (that is, the two families and the bridesmaid, and the ushers if they include friends rather than family) and let them get to know you.

One way that this may happen is at an engagement party. Many couples organise a small party with their families and perhaps some close friends to celebrate their engagement, and it would be normal for the best man and the bridesmaid to be invited as well.

Do not treat this occasion lightly. If this is the first time you will have met the other main participants in the wedding, be sure to be on your best behaviour. Their first impression of you is very important. Both sets of parents in particular will want to be sure that you are a suitable person to be the best man, and that you will act responsibly and not be an embarrassment on the wedding day. (And if the groom's parents already know you and have a rather less than flattering opinion of you, now is the time to mend your ways and show that on this occasion at least, you will take your responsibilities seriously.)

The following are key points:

- Dress appropriately for the party.
- Be on time. (If you can't be on time for this party, who is going to trust you to be on time for the wedding ceremony?)
- Do not drink too much (and do not arrive smelling of drink, either).

- Make sure everyone has a chance to get to know you.
- Do not tell inappropriate jokes and stories.

If there is no party . . .

If there is no social gathering at which you can meet the other members of the wedding party, or if for some reason you are unable to attend such a gathering, either visit both sets of parents (if that is geographically convenient) or else write to them (letters are definitely preferable to phone calls or emails for this first contact). Say how pleased and honoured you are to have been asked to be the best man, how sorry you are that you were unable to attend the engagement party (if there was one), and how much you are looking forward to meeting them at some point before the wedding.

Here again, if the groom's family in particular know little about you apart from your role in various dubious exploits that have been related to them by the groom over the years, it would be a good thing to stress that you will take your responsibilities as best man very seriously indeed. (They may not believe you, but they will nonetheless be relieved to hear it.)

The female best man

If you are a female best man, it is particularly important that you try to meet both families and make sure that everyone is happy with this unconventional arrangement. The groom's family presumably understand why you have been asked, but the bride's family may have been taken by surprise and be in need of some reassurance.

5 From 'day one' to 'three months to go'

For the purposes of this chapter and the wedding timetable in the Quick Reference section (see page 127), we will assume that you have between a year and six months to go before the wedding day. If you have less time than that, then **deal with everything in the timetable in the order in which it appears,** i.e. even if you haven't got six months to go, deal with everything in the 'twelve months to six months' section first before moving on to 'six months to three months'.

How soon should you start preparing for the wedding? There is no simple answer to that question. Obviously, if you have twelve months' notice, you can take things easier than if you only have six months' or three months' notice (or even less). But don't be complacent – no matter how much time you have, **it is never too soon to make a start to the planning.**

The first planning meeting

Very early on in the wedding preparation period, there should if at all possible be a planning meeting between the bride, the groom, the best man, and the bridesmaid. If this is not possible for some reason (e.g. because of geographical distance between you), some sort of arrangement must be made to ensure that all these key players are in touch with one another to discuss what is to happen – frequent telephone calls and/or emails will be essential.

If the others do not seem to be taking the planning side of the wedding seriously enough, you could offer yourself as the centre of communications. In that way, you will be able to prompt the others if decisions are not being made as speedily as the timetable shows they should be.

What needs to be discussed at this early stage? Almost everything. Although most of the decisions about the wedding and the reception (if there is to be one) will be made by the bride and the bride's parents and/or the groom, and will not directly involve you as best man, as the campaign manager you will need to get at least a rough idea of what is to happen as soon as possible (and the less time you have before the wedding day, the more urgent this is).

Details may of course change as the preparations progress and plans firm up, but it is never too soon to start writing in both the firm and the tentative decisions on your checklists (see pages 133–138).

From this point onwards, you should at any given time know:

* what has been completely and finally decided
* what has been tentatively agreed
* what remains to be thought out.

Nothing should be left to hope, probability, or guesswork – and it is not wise to rely on your memory either. Get everything down on paper, so that everyone (and especially you) knows what is going on. Use the checklists at the back of this book, and if you don't want to write on the book, photocopy them or write them out again in a notebook as you go along. Have the checklists and the wedding timetable with you at every planning meeting.

Helping, not interfering

While you should be involved with the planning, be careful not to interfere too much or to impose your opinions on the others. It's not your wedding, and it is for the bride and groom to make the decisions along with their parents, while your job is mainly to implement the decisions. However, if you have read this book thoroughly, there may be things needing to be done that you are aware of but the bride and groom haven't thought of. You may well be the most organised and knowledgeable member of the 'planning group', and if you don't ask certain questions or make certain suggestions, important details may be left out of the planning altogether or not brought up at an early enough stage. There is, therefore, no harm in you making the occasional suggestion, but you must be careful not to cross the line between helping and meddling.

Handling disagreements

Unfortunately, but perhaps inevitably, there may be disagreements between the bride and the groom, and you (and the bridesmaid) may have to mediate tactfully between them and keep things calm. But do be careful not to take sides – or even *seem* to take sides – in any such argument, or your relationship with the bride (who may assume that you will automatically be on the groom's side, even if you are not) may be spoiled.

Topics for the planning meeting

The first planning meeting should address the following points, though final decisions will probably not be made on all the details at this time:

- The size, style, location, and time of the wedding ceremony.
- Have the couple checked out all the legal requirements?
- Will there be a wedding planner/adviser?
- The need (if any) for ushers, and who could be asked.
- Accommodation needs.
- The style of wedding outfit the groom and the best man (and the ushers and male family members) will wear.
- Will there be an official photographer? If not, who is to take photographs, and where?
- The size, style, location, and starting and finishing times of the wedding reception.
- Transport requirements for travel to the ceremony, to the reception, and (at least for the bride and groom) from the reception.

The wedding ceremony

The size, style, and location of the wedding are generally decided by the bride and groom and the bride's parents. If not already decided, the location and time of the wedding will have to be agreed quickly and the necessary bookings made. Once you are sure of these details, you can fill them in on your checklist (page 134).

The legal requirements

Have the bride and groom checked on all the legal requirements for a valid marriage? If not – and it is not enough for them to 'think they know' – get them to check at once with the local registrar and/or the person who will be performing the ceremony. This is not something that can be left to the last minute, and if it is not done properly, the wedding will not, indeed simply cannot, take place.

The wedding planner

A bride may decide to make use of the services of a wedding planner to assist with the arrangements. This may take a lot of weight off everyone's shoulders.

The wedding planner normally liaises with the bride and her family, but as best man it would be wise if you at least made contact with them at some point nearer the wedding day.

The ushers, and who to ask

Ushers are the best man's assistants. At a small wedding, there may well be no need for ushers at all, whereas at a larger wedding, especially one held in a church, ushers will almost certainly be needed, for example to show guests to their seats and to hand out the order-of-service* sheets.

---

* Order-of-service sheets are usually decoratively printed cards or sheets of paper that show the order of the hymns, prayers, etc. in the wedding ceremony, often also with the words of the hymns.

Ushers are normally male relatives or close friends of the bride and groom, but since there could be a female best man, there is no reason at all why some or all of the ushers could not equally well be chosen from among the bride's and groom's female relatives and friends.

A full discussion of the role of the ushers at a wedding will be found in chapter eight and a short checklist in the Quick Reference section.

As best man, you should check at least three months before the wedding that the ushers have noted the date and time of the wedding in their diaries, and that there is nothing they know of that will prevent them from being available for duty.

Accommodation

Weddings usually take place in the city, town, or village in which the bride lives, and if you and the groom live in the same area, you won't have to worry about accommodation for the period of time around the wedding. But if this is not the case, then the question of who is to stay where and for how long, especially before, but also after the wedding, must be addressed (and addressed quickly, if there is not much time left until the wedding).

Among the issues to be considered are:

- Are the groom and best man going to spend the night before the wedding in the same house or hotel? (It certainly makes things easier on the morning of the wedding day if they do, as the best man will be immediately on hand to assist the groom and deal with any last-minute issues or problems that may arise. It also cuts out unnecessary travel and the risk of traffic problems and delays.)
- Can you stay with relations or friends, or will you need to book accommodation in a hotel, guest house, or bed and breakfast?
- If you will need to book accommodation, is there suitable accommodation nearby, and will there be enough for the groom, best man, and any other members of the wedding party who need it? (And do not just assume that because there is a hotel

nearby, there will be rooms available when you want them. Don't forget that hotels may be especially busy at certain times of the year. Phone or email now to check, and if necessary make a reservation.)

- At this point, when the question of accommodation is being considered, it would also be a good idea to think about the needs of the other guests. Who is coming from a distance and therefore likely to need accommodation? Where are they to stay? Is there enough accommodation close enough to the wedding venue for all those who will need it? It is not your job as best man to answer these questions, but you should ensure that the questions are at least asked. If the reception is to be held in a hotel, it may be possible to take over the whole hotel for a day or two as accommodation for the wedding party and guests if the booking is made early enough.

The photographs

It is normal practice to employ a professional photographer to take the wedding photographs, though some couples may simply ask a competent relative or friend to take the official photos. This again is something that should be decided sooner rather than later.

The bride and groom should discuss with the photographer before the wedding day what photographs they want and where and when they are to be taken. As best man, you may be called upon to help the photographer organise the groups for the photographs, so it would be a good idea to have a word with him/her at some point before the wedding to discuss the arrangements.

In addition, many couples now like to have the ceremony videoed. Although this is common practice nowadays, you should nonetheless seek the minister's or registrar's permission. Who is to do the videoing needs to be decided soon if a professional is to be booked. Where the video is to be set up needs to be discussed with the wedding venue (church, registry office, or wherever).

The wedding outfits

Depending on how long you have before the wedding day, you may not have to buy or hire your wedding clothes quite yet, but you should certainly be thinking about it. Are you and the groom (and the other men in the wedding party) to be dressed formally in, for example, morning suits, or will you all be dressed less formally in lounge suits? If in morning suits, will you be choosing black or grey? (And it is wise to bear in mind the colour of the bridesmaid's dress before this decision is made, as black suits go better with some dress colours and grey better with others.)

Chapter six deals in detail with all matters relating to the selection of suitable clothes for the wedding. You should begin to investigate local dress-hire companies to compare their prices and what they have on offer, and if possible all the outfits should have been reserved at least three months before the wedding.

The wedding reception

As with the wedding ceremony itself, the decision about the style and size of the reception traditionally rests with the bride, the groom, and the bride's parents. However, your advice may be sought as to suitable venues, and there is no harm in you giving your opinions of venues that are being considered. Possible venues should be listed and investigated at an early date, and a firm booking made as soon as possible.

Size and style of the reception

The reception can take many forms. For a legal civil marriage there is no need for more than the bride and groom and two witnesses, so the 'reception' may be no more than a meal for four in a nearby restaurant. No formal speeches (though it would be kind if someone at least toasted the bride and groom at the start of their new life together as a married couple), no dancing, and with the newly-weds simply going off quietly on their honeymoon after the meal. They may choose to hold a celebration party for family and friends at a later date.

At the other end of the scale, if the wedding ceremony has taken place in church and has been attended by a large number of family members and guests, the reception is likely to be a much grander affair, with a formal meal (and speeches) probably followed by a dance. So decisions have to be made – but not by the best man – as to the type of meal that will be provided and the probable number of guests that will have to be provided for.

Starting time

The time set for the reception to start depends on several factors. Firstly, it obviously depends on the expected finishing time of the wedding ceremony itself. Then, allowance must be made for the time it will take for the photographer to take photographs after the ceremony (and whether or not there is to be an official photographer, you can be sure that the bride's and groom's families and the other wedding guests will want to take photographs). And, after the photographs, there is the time it will take the wedding party and the guests to travel from the wedding location to the venue for the reception.

The receiving line

The actual reception meal will probably not start as soon as the wedding party and the guests reach the venue. Time must be allowed for people to greet and congratulate the bride and groom and their parents. This may be done informally, or it may involve a more formal line-up with the guests' names being called out as they arrive, and move forward to greet the members of the wedding party.

This brings us, therefore, to another possible job that the best man may have to attend to: calling out the guests' names. There are other possibilities, however. It may be decided that the best man and the bridesmaid should be in the line-up themselves, in which case some other person has to take on the role of announcing the guests. If so, who? Or it may be that the reception caterer will supply a 'master of ceremonies' for the reception, who will introduce the guests at the line-up, if necessary, and also the speakers after the meal. This is something that should be checked on when possible reception venues are considered or the booking for the reception is made.

Speeches

Traditionally, there are three speeches – by the bride's father, by the bridegroom, and by the best man. Nothing has to be finalised about the speeches at this point, but it would do no harm to consider whether anyone else might want to make a speech – the bride, perhaps, or some other member of either family.

At a formal dinner reception, the speeches come after the dinner, and are followed by the cutting of the cake by the bride and groom. However, at a more informal buffet-style reception, it may be that the cutting of the cake and the speeches precede the meal. This has to be decided.

The reception dance/entertainment

The next thing to consider is what is to happen when the meal and speeches are over. Will there be some form of entertainment? Will it include dancing? If so, what sort of dancing, and who is to provide the music for it? And has the venue enough room for this?

It is not uncommon nowadays for friends of the bride and groom who have not been invited to the wedding ceremony or the reception dinner to be invited to this later part of the reception, so the question of there being adequate room for all these extra guests must also be considered when booking a venue. And what bar facilities will be required.

Children

Some people organise some form of entertainment to keep the younger children occupied at the reception. Discuss this, and if necessary begin to make arrangements (or see that someone else does).

Venues

If the reception is not going to held at the bride's parents' house, you should begin to investigate possible venues, their facilities, charges, etc. The venue should be booked as soon as possible. (If it is being held at the bride's parents' house, you will want to investigate caterers rather than venues.)

There are many things that the bride and groom will want to ask, but as best man there are certain things that you should check:

- **Car parking**
  You should look at the size of the car park and consider whether it will hold all the guests' cars; if not, ask the manager what further parking arrangements can be made (without fear of traffic wardens or wheel-clampers). If the groom is intending to leave his car at the reception venue before the wedding, so that it is there for the couple to leave in after the reception, check where the car should be parked.

- **Master of ceremonies**
  Ask whether the venue will be supplying a master of ceremonies (because if not, you or someone else will have to take on that role). The same question should be put to caterers.

- **Music**
  If a band or DJ is being hired for the dancing after the meal, what are you going to do if they don't turn up? You may need to dance to music from CDs (which of course you will have brought with you). Check that the venue has an adequate sound system.

- **Wedding gifts**
  It is much less common than it used to be for there to be a display of the wedding presents at the reception venue, but some guests may nonetheless bring their presents with them, and they will have to be put somewhere secure, so you should definitely check on the security arrangements. (You will also want to check with the bride and groom and their parents what is to happen to the presents afterwards, since they cannot be left indefinitely at the venue.)

The time when the newly-weds leave

This will depend on the honeymoon arrangements, which may not yet have been finalised.

Transport requirements

Transport will be needed for some people at least three points on the wedding day:

- for the members of the wedding party going to the ceremony
- for the members of the wedding party between the ceremony and the reception
- for the bride and groom leaving the reception.

There may be other transport requirements.

It is usually not the best man's responsibility to organise the cars for the wedding, but you may be asked to help, or you may offer to do it. In any case, it will be up to you and the ushers to sort things out on the wedding day if adequate arrangements have not been made, so it is in your interest to make sure *before the day* that you know exactly who is going where with whom (and it would be wise to have a couple of cars with spare seats in reserve).

Going to the ceremony

Normally, if the wedding is to take place in a church, chauffeured cars are hired to take (a) the bride and her father, and (b) the bridesmaid and the bride's mother, to the ceremony. (If there are several bridesmaids and/or some flower girls and pageboys, you may need an extra car.) For a smaller ceremony, as in a registrar's office, the bride and groom may not want formal wedding cars – this has to be decided.

The groom and the best man usually travel together, in one or other's car. If the groom's car is to be used by the newly-weds when they leave the reception, it is possible that it will be parked in advance at the reception venue, and it will be the best man's car that is used. (Make sure, though, that you have a 'Plan B' to cope with the unexpected flat battery or burst tyre: e.g. the numbers of a couple of local taxi firms.) If for any reason your car is not suitable for taking yourself and the groom to the wedding, then you will need to book a hired car (with or without a chauffeur) or a taxi.

If hired cars are being booked, this needs to be done in good time. Someone needs to investigate car-hire companies, checking availability and price.

Other members of the bride's and groom's families make their own way to the ceremony (unless special arrangements are made for them) but it would be wise to consider at this early stage whether transport will be needed for anyone who does not have their own car, and to begin to think out who could give a lift to whom.

From the ceremony to the reception

The bride and groom leave in one official car, and the bridesmaid in the other. There may be a third car organised for the bride's father and mother, but nowadays they often travel in their own car.

The best man may travel with the bridesmaid, but if you need to get to the reception venue quickly you may prefer to use your own car. One or two ushers should be the last to leave the wedding venue in order to check for anything that has been left behind, and they need transport to the reception. Make sure they have a car available.

The other guests make their own way to the reception, but there are a few things to bear in mind. Some of the guests may have come to the wedding ceremony in taxis, and they may require a lift to the reception. If you are going to leave quickly for the reception, then the job of helping people find their lifts will be given to the ushers.

An alternative way of handling the transport problems that many people adopt nowadays is for a hired coach to take the guests to the reception (and back again after the reception). Some guests may prefer to use their own cars, others may be happy to go by coach.

Whatever the arrangements, well before the wedding day you should **make a list of the wedding party and all the guests, what their transport needs will be,** and how these needs will be met. (See checklist five, page 137.)

After the reception

Transport has to be arranged for the bride and groom to leave in, unless they are going away in their own car.

It might be wise at this stage to point out to the bride and groom that they will almost certainly have been drinking alcohol at the reception, and if there is any chance that they will have gone over the safe or legal limit of alcoholic consumption (and there is every likelihood that they will), then they should not be planning on driving themselves when they leave.

If guests have come to the reception by car, then they will leave in their own cars. If taxis are required, the staff at the reception venue should be able to arrange that for them. If the reception is being held at the bride's home, then a local taxi company should be warned in advance of how many taxis are likely to be needed and when. And if a coach has been hired to bring guests to the reception, then a time will also have been arranged for it to return to take the guests back to where their cars are parked. (This should, of course, be after the time at which the bride and groom will have left.)

Car hire, coach hire

You should begin to investigate local car-hire and coach companies and compare what they can offer and their prices. If possible, the bookings should be made between three and six months before the wedding.

How many planning meetings will you need?

As many as it takes to get everything organised. You will certainly need more than one meeting, but it will be up to you as the campaign manager to decide how many meetings are needed, and when.

The key thing is to **make sure that all the decisions are made in good time**, but how many meetings that will take can only be decided by you. Get the team together or, failing that, make sure everyone is in frequent contact through you, to review progress. Look over the wedding timetable and the checklists regularly to see that nothing has been missed.

Other things to attend to

Start a contacts file

As decisions are made about the wedding venue, reception venue, car-hire company, and so on, you should enter all these details in your contacts file.

Checklist one (page 134) provides you with a list of all the 'main players' in the wedding. Whether or not you know the people involved, get their details down in a contacts file as soon as you can.

Find out about the families, family customs, and family politics

Over the next few months, try to get to know the names and faces of close members of both families. Commit this information to memory and you will do a far better job when it comes to the big group photographs and introductions at the reception.

At some point, you should also inquire (tactfully) about any family customs, or any family politics about which you need to be aware. Family politics is of particular importance for a day on which people who may not be on the best of terms will be obliged to be in the same room as one another and alcohol will be flowing. For example, it is a fact of modern life that some of the guests at a wedding (and perhaps the bride's or groom's parents) may be divorced couples, perhaps with new partners of their own. Will they be on speaking terms? Or again, does Aunt X not speak to Aunt Y because of something Uncle Y was supposed to have said or done thirty years ago? Is there someone who has a drink problem (or worse)?

It would be a wise best man who acquainted himself with family issues such as these, so that he knew which people should be kept an eye on, kept apart, or not even mentioned to each other. (But if you note these things down, be *very* careful where you put your notes. The idea is to prevent fights, not start them!)

Start thinking about the stag party

The stag party may take quite a bit of organisation, so it would be wise to start thinking about this soon. Chapter nine covers all you need to know about planning a stag party.

If you (with or without the groom) are not going to organise the stag party on your own, get in touch with two or three close friends of yours and the groom's, and get the stag party planning underway. Depending on what is planned, you may need to make bookings pretty soon.

Start thinking about your speech

It is never too soon to make a start on this, so get a notebook and start jotting down ideas, anecdotes, jokes, etc. Keep the speech constantly at the back of your mind and you will be surprised how many ideas you get (even if you reject most of them in the end).

6 What to wear

What you and the groom will wear for the wedding will be decided by the groom in consultation with the bride . . . and possibly the groom's mother! Hopefully, you will be asked for your opinion as well. If not, don't be offended; just go with the decision that the others have made.

The choice of menswear for weddings is pretty simple: you can dress formally in morning dress (or, in certain circumstances, dinner jacket), or informally, for example in lounge suits. (Highland dress is also a possibility to be considered.) An exception would be if the ceremony was being held somewhere where some sort of special clothing would be required – on a beach, for example, or in a swimming pool. And of course, since there is no *legal* requirement to be 'respectably' dressed for a wedding, especially at a registry office, the bride and groom can choose to be as informal or off-the-wall as they like. (However, if the groom wants the two of you to dress in something really ridiculous, dissuade him. What may have seemed a great idea that evening in the pub will almost certainly not amuse the bride, or the groom's mother, on the day, and will embarrass the groom *forever* afterwards. You're his friend – for his sake, say 'no' firmly.)

Generally, the other men in the wedding party (the bride's father, the groom's father, the bride's and groom's brothers, and the ushers) follow the lead of the groom and the best man, and dress in a similar style.

Formal or informal?

The decision on whether to wear formal or informal dress will depend to a certain extent on the venue for and formality of the wedding, and the style of dress being worn by the bride and bridesmaid. At a church wedding, for example, if the bride is dressed in a white gown and the bridesmaid is also wearing a formal gown, then the groom and best man would probably be expected to be formally dressed as well. If, on the other hand, the bride and bridesmaid are less formally dressed, perhaps in suits – as is usually the case with a second marriage and generally the case when the marriage is taking place at a registry office – the groom and best man should also be dressed in lounge suits rather than morning dress.

Morning dress or evening dress?

Generally one wears morning dress as formal wear at a wedding, even if it is taking place in the afternoon. But if the wedding is taking place in the late afternoon, with a late reception, then dinner jackets are acceptable. (But in this case, the fact that evening dress rather than morning dress is to be worn should be intimated to all male members of the family and male guests. Some guests might be embarrassed to be wearing a different style of formal wear from what the groom and best man are wearing, and a mixture of styles will not look good in the photographs.)

Morning dress: hiring your wedding outfit

There was a time when formal morning dress and evening dress were part of many men's wardrobes, but these days are gone, so it is almost certain that you and the groom (and the other men in the wedding party) will be hiring your wedding outfits.

Choose a reputable dress-hire firm and go along well before the wedding to try on and reserve your suits (see the wedding timetable, page 127). If you have time, check out all the dress-hire companies in your area, especially their stock and their prices, before making your choice.

It's a good idea to try to arrange for all the men's fittings to be done together, or failing that at least by the same company. (You may even get a discount if you bring in the fathers, the brothers, and the ushers as well.) Since you and the groom will be together for much of the day, it would certainly be a good idea for the two of you to go together to hire your suits, so that you can be fitted together and choose suitable matching ties, handkerchiefs, etc.

If all the fittings cannot be done at the same time, it is up to you as best man to make sure that the rest of the men know what style of dress they are supposed to be wearing and, if necessary, where to go to hire it.

Make sure that your suit fits well and is comfortable. While you should certainly take the advice of the experienced dress-hire assistant, do not accept anything that you are not entirely happy with. You're going to be in these clothes all day: you need to be comfortable as well as looking smart. Depending on the date of the wedding, take the probable weather conditions into account, and check that the outfit will be warm enough on a cold day but comfortable on a hot day.

It is always best that you and the groom go in person to collect your suits, so that you can try them on before leaving the shop. (This is especially true if alterations have been required – it would be disastrous to discover on the morning of the wedding day that the alterations hadn't been made as intended.) It will probably be your job to return the groom's suit along with your own on the day after the wedding.

Grey or black?

Morning suits are available in a range of colours, but those worn at weddings are generally grey or black. Grey morning dress consists of a grey tailcoat, grey waistcoat, and grey trousers; black morning dress consists of a black tailcoat, a grey waistcoat, and black pinstripe trousers.

Normally the groom and the best man will wear identical or very similar outfits. If you aren't going to do this, then a best man should not choose to wear anything unusual (such as a green or brown suit) without consulting the groom (and the bride, just to be on the safe side). If you are wearing green or brown when all the other men are in black or grey, you will be the one to stand out rather than the groom, which would be quite inappropriate on *his* wedding day.

Given the standard choice between grey and black, what should influence your decision? There are two factors that may be taken into consideration:

- the time of year
- the ladies' colour scheme.

The time of year

It doesn't really matter, and there is certainly no hard and fast rule, but many people feel that grey looks better at a summer wedding and black better at a winter wedding. (Though with British weather, it could be hard to decide what season to dress for!)

The ladies' colour scheme

Much more important than dressing for the season is to take account of the colour of the bridesmaid's dress or suit (and the bride's, if she is not wearing white). If the ladies are wearing strong colours, then black morning dress might be better than grey, whereas grey might go better than black with paler shades. This needs to be discussed at a planning meeting, and it might even be worth while taking samples of the dress material with you (if that is possible) to the clothes-hire shop when you go to choose your suits.

Shirts

With black morning dress, shirts are usually white. There are variety of styles available, and the best thing is to choose something you and the groom like and that goes with the suits. Two factors to keep in mind are **comfort** and **look**.

- Firstly, make sure that the shirt fits comfortably, especially round the neck, as you will be wearing it with the collar fastened for the whole day, including the dancing at the reception. (It is *not* the done thing to loosen your tie and collar while wearing morning dress.)

- Secondly, if the shirt has a winged collar, make sure that the collar will withstand the warm, sweaty conditions and activities of the day without drooping. If in doubt, opt for a collar that folds down.

With grey morning dress, a wider range of shirt colours is possible, but when making your choice be sure to keep the ladies' dress colours in mind.

Waistcoats

Waistcoats are generally grey, but you can, if you choose, add a touch of colour to your outfit by going for something brighter and more colourful. You and the groom can choose either to have matching waistcoats or waistcoats that do not match. Some people in fact suggest that it can be a good idea for the groom and the best man to have waistcoats of a different colour to those of the ushers and the other men in the wedding party, so that you stand out from the crowd.

Don't forget that with waistcoats, as with other colourful items of your clothing, you should choose a shade that does not clash with the bride's and bridesmaid's colour scheme.

Ties and cravats

With black morning coats, wedding ties are most often silver-grey. With grey morning coats, a wider range of colours is possible, of course taking into account the colours of your shirt and waistcoat. **One colour to avoid in ties is, of course, black.** That's for funerals.

As an alternative to a tie, you might choose to wear a cravat. The colour choices are essentially the same as for ties, and there are a variety of styles. You can buy or hire cravats that you tie yourself, but tying them takes practice: perhaps it would be better to opt for a pre-tied cravat and save a lot of hassle on the morning of the wedding day. (If you are wearing a cravat, you will probably need a cravat pin.)

Socks and shoes

With black or grey morning dress, socks and shoes should be black.

Handkerchiefs

Buy something to match your tie or cravat. Otherwise, white.

Top hat and gloves

Opinions vary about the need for a top hat and gloves. At a *very* formal church ceremony, you and the groom may want to have them, though you will not actually wear them at any point, but otherwise they are really just an encumbrance which you would be far better off without. And why waste money hiring something you don't need?

Hats may be required, however, by certain religious groups. Find out before you hire your morning dress.

... and one final point about morning dress

The jacket buttons of a morning coat should always be left unfastened.

Dinner jackets

Little needs to be said about evening dress. It normally consists of a black jacket and black trousers, sometimes with a cummerbund round the waist. Shoes and socks are black. The shirt is white, and a variety of styles are available.

With a dinner jacket, you wear a bow tie. Bow ties may be black, but there is no reason not to choose something brighter. As with morning dress, your colour choice should take into account the colours of the bride's and bridesmaid's outfits. You can buy or hire bow ties that you tie yourself, but why bother? It is much easier to get a clip-on, pre-tied bow tie, and avoid the trouble on the wedding day. If you are hiring a bow tie, make sure that the one you are getting is not the worse for wear: it might be better to invest in buying one of your own.

As with bow ties, cummerbunds allow for some colour to be brought into the picture, as they need not be black.

Military uniform

If you and the groom are in the armed forces, you may want to wear dress uniform for the wedding ceremony.

Informal wear: lounge suits

The first question to ask yourself is: do I need a new suit? If yes, then presumably you are going to buy one.

You probably have your own lounge suit already, so you hardly need to be told how to choose one for the wedding. Obviously there is a wide range of styles and colours from which you could choose, so you should consult the groom in order that your outfits complement each other. And remember, it is his wedding day, so you do not want to wear something that would make you stand out more than the groom in the photos. Look smart but keep it low-key, unless you and the groom together decide otherwise.

Before buying, you also need to decide what colour to choose (taking into consideration what the groom will be wearing, and of course the bride and bridesmaid). You might also be wise to think about what use you will hope to get from the suit after the wedding – that purple suit, while stunning at the wedding, might just not be suitable for everyday wear to the office.

Be particularly careful to choose a suit that fits well and is comfortable. You may want to pay a little more than you usually do for a suit, since this is a special occasion, and you must leave enough time for any alterations that are required, so do not delay in looking around in the shops. Complete the outfit with a shirt, tie, socks and shoes of suitable colours, and a coloured handkerchief, matching the tie, for your breast pocket (again taking into account the colour scheme of the outfits the bride and bridesmaid will be wearing).

Highland dress

If you and the groom want to wear kilts for the wedding, go to a dress-hire company who are experienced in hiring out Highland dress.

There are a number of matters to be decided:

- Do you and the groom want to wear the same tartan or not? It is not vital that one wears a tartan associated with one's own family name, though you or he may prefer to; nowadays there are also tartans associated with countries, towns, football teams, and so on. And you can get very smart kilts that are not in tartan at all (black kilts, blue kilts, leather kilts, etc.).
- The colours of the tartan(s) you choose should take into account the colours of the bride's and bridesmaid's dresses.
- Make sure that your kilt is of the correct length. There may be worse things seen in wedding photographs than a bridegroom and a best man wearing badly fitting kilts, but there aren't many. Remember that you and the groom are going to spend important parts of the day standing next to one another, so go together to hire your kilts, and when you try them on, stand beside one another in front of a mirror and see how you look. If you are not absolutely 100% happy with your appearance, abandon the kilt idea and hire suits instead.
- And finally, no matter what you have heard about what Scotsmen traditionally wear under their kilts, anyone wearing a kilt at a wedding should also wear something appropriate underneath (if possible in a colour matching the kilt), so that there are no embarrassing moments.

In formal wear, the jackets worn with kilts are not dissimilar to dinner jackets, and are usually black with black waistcoats (though other colours are available to match some of the less traditional kilt colours). Shirts come in a variety of styles, but are usually white, and worn with a black bow tie. Coloured ties and white lace jabots are possible options with certain styles of jacket. In less formal wear, jackets are often of tweed and shirts are again usually white, but in an even more informal style where no jacket is to be worn, then a wide variety of colours and styles of shirt is available. Appropriate socks and shoes (brogues) should be worn. And you need a decorative kilt pin, a belt, and of course a sporran! In all these and related matters, ask the hire company to advise you and show you what they have available. Alternatively, go online, google 'Highland dress', and take a look at the possibilities, which are too many to be listed here.

Clothes for the female best man

At a formal wedding, a female best man *might* wear a dress similar in style to that of the bridesmaid, but that is probably not a good idea (she would simply look like another bridesmaid), and it would be better if she wore a dress and jacket or a suit such as she would have worn had she simply been a guest at the wedding. It is probably better not to have a dress or suit of exactly the same shade as the bridesmaid's, but of course the colours chosen should not clash either. At a civil ceremony or a second marriage, where the bride will probably wear a suit rather than a wedding dress, the bridesmaid and the female best man will do likewise.

Just as the best man should not outshine the bridegroom on his wedding day, you should take care not to upstage the bride, so dress appropriately and attractively, but not provocatively. It is not the day for you to set out to attract attention to yourself.

A female best man might choose to wear a man's suit of the same style as the one being worn by the bridegroom, as a male best man would do. While there is nothing specifically against this, it would be wise to check in advance with both families, and with the minister, that this will be acceptable and will cause no offence. (The very fact of there being a female best man might itself cause a few raised eyebrows, and in some religious circles a woman wearing men's clothing at a wedding ceremony would definitely not be acceptable.) A trouser suit might be a satisfactory compromise.

Final-night preparations

When you have got all your wedding clothes ready and are looking them over on the evening before the wedding, check if anything needs ironing (the shirt, for example), hang the suit and shirt neatly to prevent creasing, and give your shoes a good polish. Check that the groom does the same.

... and definitely not final-night preparations

No matter how smart your clothes are, the overall effect is going to be spoiled if you are having a bad hair day. You don't want untidy hair at the wedding, but on the other hand you don't want to turn up with a just-cut-yesterday look either. You should know yourself how long before the wedding day you need to get your hair cut so that it looks perfect on the day (probably about a week to ten days), so get this into your wedding timetable now.

Buttonholes and corsages

A buttonhole is a flower that the men in the wedding party wear in the buttonhole of their jackets or, more usually, pinned to the lapel. However, it will almost certainly be the bride who chooses the colour and type of flower.

It is no longer expected that the groom and best man will wear white carnations, as was traditional in the past. Nowadays a much wider range of flowers is available and acceptable: red or pink carnations, roses, sprigs of white heather, etc. You and the groom might want to choose something even more exotic – orchids, for example, can make quite stunning buttonholes, which will certainly make you and the groom stand out, though of course they will also be more expensive. Check with the florist before the flowers are ordered to see what might be available.

Rather than a buttonhole, a female best man should wear a corsage, as do the other principal ladies at a wedding, unless of course she has opted to dress in menswear, in which case she should have a buttonhole like the men in the wedding party.

As best man, it is your responsibility to ensure that you, the groom, the ushers, and the groom's parents and family all have their buttonholes and corsages. You may need to pick them up from the florist, or ensure that someone else does, on the morning of the wedding. Alternatively, they may be delivered to the bride's home or her parent's home (depending on where she is leaving from) along with the bride's and bridesmaid's bouquets, or the florist may deliver them to the reception venue along with the table decorations. In either case, they must be collected and taken to the wedding venue. It may be that they will be delivered directly to the venue, which saves a lot of hassle.

The key thing for you to do, a few days before the wedding, is to contact the florist and find out exactly what the delivery arrangements are. You can then make the necessary arrangements for you (or perhaps better still, one of the ushers, as you have enough to do on the wedding day already) to pick up the flowers and take them to the wedding venue, where they can be handed out to the members of the wedding party as they arrive.

Who pays for what?

This could be a delicate matter. While in the past the groom traditionally paid for the hiring of the best man's outfit as well as his own (and sometimes also the ushers' suits), practice is changing, and usually each person now pays for his own clothes hire. You certainly should not simply *expect* that the groom will pay for your suit as well as his own, and it would be a nice gesture if you *offered* to pay for the hire of yours.

If you are buying a lounge suit, which you will be keeping for your own use after the wedding, you pay for it (and all the accessories, unless the groom offers to buy them). The same would apply in the case of a female best man.

It is the groom who pays for the buttonholes for himself, the best man, and the ushers.

7 Invitations and wedding presents

The invitation

Although you have obviously already been invited to the wedding by virtue of having been asked to be the best man, you will almost certainly also get a formal invitation from the bride's parents some weeks before the wedding. Although you know and they know that you will be attending the wedding, it would be discourteous not to reply to this invitation.

So, you should reply to the invitation as soon as you receive it. Your reply should be in the form of a letter, not an email, and certainly not just a telephone call. Even if you happen to meet the bride's parents and thank them for the invitation, you should still out of courtesy send a written acceptance.

Invitations are generally written (or printed on formal invitation cards) in a formal style along the lines of:

Mr and Mrs Charles Smith
request the pleasure of the company of
Mr Peter Brown
at the wedding of their daughter Julie
to Mr John Jones
at St Stephen's Church, Oldfield,
on Saturday 10th March at 3 p.m.

It is normal to reply in a similar formal style, repeating all the details as they appear on the invitation:

Mr Peter Brown thanks Mr and Mrs Charles Smith for their kind invitation to the wedding of their daughter Julie to Mr John Jones at St Stephen's Church, Oldfield, on Saturday 10th March at 3 p.m., and has great pleasure in accepting the invitation.

If you write a formal reply like this, you do not sign it.

However, if you really feel this style of reply is too formal and old-fashioned, and you are not comfortable with it, a more informal acceptance will generally suffice (with perhaps some additional remark about you being honoured to be the best man and looking forward to the wedding, etc.):

Dear Mr and Mrs Smith,

Thank you very much for your kind invitation to Julie and John's wedding, which I am very pleased to accept.

I was very honoured to be asked by John to be his best man, and I am looking forward to meeting you all at the wedding rehearsal.

Yours sincerely,

Replying on behalf of your partner

If you have a fiancée, wife, or long-term partner, she may be invited along with you. Her invitation will be part of your invitation, and you should reply on her behalf as well as your own:

Mr Peter Brown thanks Mr and Mrs Charles Smith for their kind invitation to himself and Miss Fiona Green to the wedding of their daughter Julie to Mr John Jones at St Stephen's Church, Oldfield on Saturday 10th March at 3p.m. and has great pleasure in accepting the invitation.

Or, more informally:

Dear Mr and Mrs Smith,

Thank you very much for your kind invitation to Fiona and

myself to attend Julie and John's wedding, which we are very pleased to accept.

I was very honoured to be asked by John to be his best man, and Fiona and I are both looking forward very much to meeting you and the rest of your family at the wedding.

Yours sincerely,

Someone who has only recently become your girlfriend will very probably *not* be invited to the wedding. It depends to some extent on the style and formality of the reception: she would be less likely to be invited to a formal meal than, say, to a light buffet. If she is invited, you may get an invitation to you 'and guest'. It is also possible that she will receive a separate invitation, in which case each of you replies separately.

If your girlfriend is not invited, do not take offence, and do not make an issue of it. However, since it is now quite common practice for couples to extend an invitation to a wider circle of friends to the evening dance after the reception meal, your girlfriend might well be invited to that part of the reception. You could tactfully ask for this, but don't forget that you are still the best man and will have certain responsibilities throughout the evening.

Children

If a couple is invited to the wedding, it doesn't follow automatically that their children are. If it is not clear whether your children are included in the invitation, check in good time so that you can make arrangements for them to be looked after if necessary. Children who are old enough may be invited to the dance after the meal.

The wedding gift

As a guest at the wedding, you would be buying a present for the bride and groom in any case. As best man, however, you will probably want to buy a slightly more expensive present than you would have done if you were simply a guest.

Choose your gift thoughtfully, but be imaginative. Should it be something practical for the home or something luxurious or frivolous that the bride and groom might not buy for themselves? (If the bride and groom are not having a honeymoon, you might even pay for them to have a short holiday somewhere.) **Whatever you choose, remember that you are buying a gift for the *couple*, not for the groom alone.**

The wedding list

Many couples nowadays have already been living together for some time or, even if not together, in their own homes rather than their parents' homes. Since they are likely to have many things that would once have been considered suitable wedding gifts (pots and pans, cutlery, crockery, bedding, towels), many couples help with the choice of suitable gifts by making a wedding list, which shows what sort of things they still need and would like to receive. The list may be kept at a department store (where it can be consulted) or it may be held by the bride or her parents (from whom it can be borrowed).

Do not feel pressurised, just because you are the best man, into buying something that is really out of your price range. It *is* a special occasion, and you *are* the best man, but there is no need to get into debt, and certainly no need to show off to others how well-off or generous you are. The giving of gifts is not a competition.

If you are married or living with a long-term partner, you and your partner should give a joint gift. However, a fiancée or a girlfriend may feel that she wants to give a separate gift herself, especially if she has received a separate invitation, rather than giving a gift jointly with you. Either way is entirely acceptable.

8 The ushers and their duties

The ushers at a wedding are the best man's assistants. Or, looked at from the opposite direction, the best man, as the wedding campaign manager, is in charge of the team of ushers.

Who to choose?

Generally the ushers are chosen from among the brothers, close relatives, or close friends of the bride and groom. (Of course, just as there can be female best men, there is no reason why there should not be female ushers.) The best man, however, will generally be involved in their selection.

It is always better if ushers will have no other responsibilities on the wedding day (such as small children, heavily pregnant wives, or elderly relatives who may require their attention), so that they are free to deal at a moment's notice with any task or problem that might arise. Ideally they should be familiar with (or have familiarised themselves with) the location of both the wedding venue and the reception venue, as they may be called upon to give directions to, or provide a taxi service for, other guests. Ideally, therefore, they should be able to drive and have available transport.

How many ushers?

Traditionally, there were the same number of ushers as bridesmaids, so that the ushers could be escorts to the bridesmaids. Since escorts are no longer considered essential, and ushers and bridesmaids may have partners of their own in any case, this is no longer considered essential. (Nevertheless, the best man should always ensure that any bridesmaid who does not have a partner is looked after throughout the day, and with this in mind it would be kind to ensure that for any unpartnered bridesmaid there is an usher or other male friend who is free to be her partner for the day and especially the evening dance.)

Usually four or five ushers are enough for even the largest wedding, though particular circumstances may require even more. For a smaller wedding, one or two ushers may be quite enough. And if the wedding is taking place in a registry office, there will be no need for ushers at all (though it may still be useful to have at least one friend or relative stationed outside in the street to deal with problems or answer questions – such as 'Where is the nearest car park?' – or even just to reassure guests that they have come to the right place).

The ushers' duties

The ushers' exact duties will vary from wedding to wedding, and will depend on the size, formality, and location of the wedding ceremony. The exact requirements should be discussed at a planning meeting well in advance of the wedding day, so that the number of ushers needed can be decided, and friends and relatives approached and signed up in good time.

Being an usher is not a great responsibility, but if the job is done properly, it helps the day go smoothly and removes various burdens from the best man's shoulders.

The ushers' main duties are as follows (assuming, for the moment, a church wedding):

Before the ceremony

- The ushers should be at the church before any other guests, therefore probably (to be on the safe side) about forty-five minutes to an hour before the start of the ceremony.

- Ushers assist the guests with the parking of their cars, either by ensuring that cars are parked sensibly and safely in the church car park or in the street outside, or by directing guests to a nearby car park or suitable nearby street. One or two ushers should be sufficient for this. (The ushers should be warned not to let your car get boxed in by other guests' cars, as you may need to leave for the reception promptly after the ceremony.)

- Ushers greet guests at the church door, direct the guests to their correct places in the church, and hand out the order-of-service sheets (or hymn books). In very formal weddings, ushers may be expected to escort guests to their places, but this is probably not necessary at most weddings, except in the case of elderly, frail, and disabled guests. However, when the mother of the bride arrives, she should be escorted to her seat by an usher.

- In case of inclement weather (this is Britain, after all!), the ushers on car park and door duty should all be equipped with umbrellas to shelter guests as they leave their cars or taxis to enter the church.

- One of the ushers may be deputed to collect the buttonholes and corsages for the wedding party, and if so will be responsible for distributing them as each person arrives at the church.

- Another usher may have been deputed to collect the order-of-service sheets from the printer, from the bride's house, or from wherever they are on the morning of the wedding. The ushers hand these out as guests arrive. (Make sure that order-of-service sheets are placed at the front of the church before the ceremony, for you, the groom, the bride, the bride's father, the bridesmaid, and any other bride's attendants.)

- One usher should have the responsibility of letting the groom and best man know when the bride and her father arrive at the church door.

After the ceremony

- Ushers may help the best man and the photographer organise the people for the wedding photographs. They can also help the official photographer by ensuring that enthusiastic amateurs are not getting in the way.
- If the church does not permit the throwing of confetti (and many do not nowadays), the ushers should keep an eye on the guests and tactfully ask anyone who is carrying confetti not to throw it.
- The ushers supervise the car park traffic again, and if necessary direct guests from the wedding venue to the reception venue. If guests need transport from the church to the reception, ushers should direct them to the cars in which they will be travelling (this having been worked out beforehand).
- One or two ushers should go back into the church after everyone has left, in order to pick up articles that guests may have left behind and take them to the reception where they can be returned to their owners.

At the reception

- While some of the ushers remain at the church, one or two ushers should make their way to the reception venue, where again they can supervise parking, shelter guests under umbrellas, etc.
- As guests arrive, the ushers may then help the best man in offering drinks to guests (though the reception venue staff may be doing this), introducing guests to one another, and making sure no one is left standing alone in the crowd.
- Later in the evening, the ushers should, like the best man, dance with as many female guests as possible (while, of course, not neglecting their own partners).

The best man's responsibilities

Your responsibility as best man is to make sure that the ushers each know exactly what *their* responsibilities are, and that they are always in the right place at the right time. Since your main responsibility at the church is to be with and support the bridegroom, it would be sensible to appoint one of the ushers as 'chief usher', your official deputy, so that there is someone who can supervise the other ushers and make decisions or deal with problems when you are not available.

If there is a wedding rehearsal, the ushers should attend so they can see the layout of the building, where the toilets are (someone is bound to ask on the day), what the car parking arrangements will be, whether there are 'blind spots' in the church (behind pillars, for example) where guests should not be seated, and so on. If that is not possible, then you should note all these details and then the groom, the best man, and the ushers should have a meeting sometime during the week preceding the wedding to go over the wedding details. (You may all meet at the stag party, but that is hardly the time to discuss the arrangements for the wedding.)

In either case, you should **make out a written wedding plan for each usher**, detailing who is doing what when, so that nothing gets missed and everyone knows what their responsibilities are. Whatever you do, do not leave it all to the morning of the wedding, as you will have far too much to do.

It is also the best man's job to ensure that the ushers know what style of clothes to wear to the wedding, and have hired their outfits in good time.

Seating arrangements

One thing the ushers must know is the seating arrangements in the church.

Obviously, the front seats must be reserved for the main participants in the wedding. Behind them sit the close family and close friends, and behind them the other guests. The basic rule is: **the closer the family connection, the further forward the guest sits.**

The groom's parents sit in the second pew from the front **on the**

right-hand side. If there are divorced parents, decide in advance how to seat them and warn the ushers. Normally, if parents are divorced but not remarried, they are seated together. If they are divorced and remarried, they may want to sit in separate pews.

The bride's mother sits in the front pew **on the left-hand side** of the aisle, leaving an empty seat on her right for her husband to join her when he has given away the bride. The bridesmaid and any other attendants normally stay where they are during the ceremony, but alternatively all but the chief bridesmaid may sit in the pew behind the bride's parents.

Traditionally, the **bride's family and friends sit on the left-hand side** of the church (facing the altar), and the **groom's sit on the right-hand side.** Ushers therefore ask guests as they arrive which family they are related to – 'Bride or groom?'. However, if one side of the church is clearly becoming much fuller than the other side, the ushers would do well to try to avoid a noticeable imbalance by directing people to fill the emptier side regardless of whose friends or relatives they are. No one is likely to be offended by this (but if anyone is, they should of course be allowed to sit where they want). And since many couples have been together for some time before their marriage, they may have friends in common, and these guests can be directed towards the emptier side of the church. At many weddings nowadays, the question of family relationship is simply ignored, and guests sit where they choose.

Other factors that the ushers may want to bear in mind is that elderly guests may want to be near the front of the church so that they can see and hear what is going on, or else nearer the back of the church so that they can slip out easily if they need to. Guests with babies and young children should, perhaps, also be seated nearer the back of the church, and at the end of a row, so that they too can slip out if need be, without disrupting the service. On the other hand, parents of flower girls and pageboys should be seated fairly near the front and at the end of a row, so that they can quickly deal with tears and tantrums if need be.

The ushers sit near the back or entrance of the church so that they are in a convenient place to deal with latecomers or anyone who suddenly has to leave. There should always be room near the door of the church for latecomers, and it would be wise to have one or more of the ushers seated near the door to silently greet anyone who arrives late, direct them to a seat, and hand them an order-of-service sheet.

Behind the official guests, or off to one side, or perhaps on a balcony, depending on the design of the church, there may be friends and neighbours who have not been officially invited to the wedding but who have come along nevertheless to take part in the service.

9 The stag party and other celebrations

Traditionally, a stag party probably just meant a 'stag night'; a few drinks in a pub with some friends on the groom's supposed 'last night of freedom', or perhaps a meal in a local restaurant, or a visit to a night club. It might even have been held in someone's house. There might have been a kissogram girl or a stripper, but that was about it. But stag parties have changed. They are no longer mere stag *nights* – they are often stag *events*, stag *weekends*, stag *holidays*, with the groom and his friends heading off somewhere – in the UK, on the continent, or even further afield (think New York, Las Vegas, or Florida) – sometimes to take part in organised action activities such as paintballing, quad biking, snowboarding or tank driving.

So the stag party, once upon a time relatively simple and straightforward – go to pub, enjoy party, get groom home safely – may now actually be the most demanding part of the whole wedding campaign.

If there is going to be a stag party of some sort (it's not obligatory), what must be decided?

• What sort of event is it to be and where is it going to be held?
• Are you going to consult the groom about it or surprise him?
• When should the stag party be held?
• Who is going to organise it?
• Who to invite?

What sort of event is it to be and where is it going to be held?

Are you going to have a simple stag night out (or even a stag night in, at someone's house), or are you thinking of an activities event in the UK, or a trip abroad?

- Firstly, it's the groom's stag party, so **choose something *he* would enjoy.**
- Secondly, **time** may be a deciding factor. How long have you got before the wedding to get something organised? If it is just a few drinks or a meal with some friends, then there is little need for planning far in advance, though you may need to book a restaurant or a room in a pub in good time. But if you are thinking of a weekend or holiday away, with organised activities, you can't begin too soon. Bookings may have to be made well ahead of time. Is there enough time left?
- **Cost** is another factor to be considered. Even a weekend in Europe could make a sizeable hole in participants' pockets, though places such as the Baltic states or the Czech Republic are relatively cheap. A weekend of organised activity in the UK may not be cheap either, once travel, accommodation, food and drinks, and the cost of the activities themselves are taken into account. Could this prevent some people taking part? If so, you may want to opt for something less exciting and adventurous, but also less expensive. The cheapest option is, of course, simply to hold a party in someone's home, with drinks bought in bulk, glasses hired, etc. (The additional benefit is that if anyone is not fit to go home, they can stay where they are for the night.)

Is it to be a surprise for the groom?

If you are not going to tell the groom until the last minute what you have planned, you may be more limited in your choice of what you can do and where you can go. On the other hand, you could simply tell him to keep a particular weekend free, and to make sure his passport is valid, but tell him nothing more about where you are taking him or what he will be doing.

When should the stag party be held?

That depends on what is planned. But whatever you do, **do not hold any stag party on the day before the wedding,** even if that means that guests coming from some distance away for the wedding itself may miss the party. You don't want the groom, the best man, the ushers, and many of the male guests to be half-asleep and hungover on the day.

Similarly, a trip abroad should be held at least a week before the wedding. Do not plan to arrive back on the morning of, or even the day before, the ceremony – too many things can go wrong. A strike of air traffic controllers or a sudden terrorist threat, and you, the groom, and your friends could find yourselves stuck in an airport in the middle of Europe when you should be at the wedding.

Who is to organise the event?

Traditionally it is the best man who organises the stag party, but if you intend to organise something more than a simple stag night out on the town, you would be well advised to set up a small team with two or three friends to handle this together, even if as best man you have overall control and responsibility. It will, of course, involve more planning meetings. (If the stag night/weekend/holiday is to be a surprise for the groom, he will obviously not be involved; if not a surprise, he should be involved.)

Organising the stag event or stag weekend will require more than just meetings. Someone will have to research possible activities and holiday centres (try googling – for example, look for 'stag events'), organise the travel and accommodation, and keep all the participants informed throughout the planning period. There will be frequent phone calls and emails, and possibly visits to travel agents. (Though much can be done online these days, it may be easier to involve the professionals and let them deal with the bulk of the admin.) You can get relatively cheap all-in package deals, so hunt around.

If you really don't have time to attend to all this, step back and pass the buck to someone reliable who has.

The key thing is that the stag party, whatever it may involve, should be properly organised.

Who comes to the stag party?

Obviously, you do, and the groom does. Beyond that, it can be any thing from a small group to a large party. It may be left to the groom to choose who is to join the party, or it may be organised as a surprise for him. The ushers are invited, as well as the bride's and groom's brothers and close male relatives, and close male friends of the groom. Some of these may be unable to attend, especially those who are already having to travel a long way to attend the wedding itself, but they should still be invited.

The groom may issue the invitations himself, or he may ask you to deal with this on his behalf. There is no need for formal invitations to be sent out; invitations are usually passed on informally, by word of mouth, email, letter, or even a notice stuck up on the office noticeboard (though if you do this, it may be hard to stop the uninvited joining in).

Factors to consider

There are a number of things to bear in mind when making up the list of invitees:

- Will everyone get on together? Will anyone feel left out? Will there be cliques? The bride's brothers may, after all, have nothing in common with the guys from the office or the rugby club, even though the groom and you get on well with all of them. (This may be particularly important for a stag weekend or holiday, where people are going to be together for more than a few hours, and can't get away from each other.)

- Is everyone you are thinking of inviting likely to enjoy the same sort of party/event? For a start, some people drink more than others. And not everyone wants to go go-karting in Wales or clubbing in Barcelona.

If one stag night or stag event is really not going to work, you perhaps need to organise more than one, catering for different groups. Or, as at many wedding receptions, there could be a main event for a small number of people, with others invited to join in later on. And if you, the groom, and a small number of friends are having an activity holiday away from home, it might be a good idea to organise some sort of get-together locally for other friends and colleagues. (It might also be a good idea to hold a get-together *before* the trip for all those who will be taking part, so that they can get to know one another.)

Are the fathers invited?

Traditionally both the father of the groom and the father of the bride were invited to the stag night, often in the fervent hope that they would decline the invitation or at most come for a couple of drinks and then leave early. It is probably the case nowadays that fathers do not expect to be invited along to a stag night, and certainly do not expect to be invited to a stag weekend away.

To a great extent, though, it depends on the fathers themselves. Would they fit in with the rest of the staggers or not? And does the groom want his father and his future father-in-law to be at his stag party in any case? Whatever decision is made, it would certainly be wrong to invite one father and not the other. It's definitely a case of both or neither.

Does anyone make a speech?

At a stag party, there is no need for a speech at all. But as best man, you may nonetheless want, or be asked, to say a few words. The emphasis should be on the 'few'.

Be prepared. Have some anecdotes ready, and a few jokes. (At a stag party, you can say things about the groom and tell jokes that would be totally inappropriate at the wedding reception.) But remember, if people have been drinking, do not say anything that could start an argument or a fight.

Who pays for what?

Here again, tradition says one thing but modern practice differs. Often, in the past, the groom would pay, since it was technically he who was inviting his friends out. Or else it was the best man who paid, since he had organised the party on behalf of the groom. However, nowadays, with prices as they are, that could place a severe financial burden on a groom or best man. So for a stag night involving a meal or drinks out somewhere, it is usual that the costs are shared. It may be that the groom will pay for part of the evening and the guests for the rest, or else the guests may cover all their own costs and in addition spread the groom's share between them. At a pub, you as best man might buy the first round of drinks, and then others would buy later rounds.

You as best man, or whoever is organising the event if it is not you, should make sure that everyone knows in advance what they will be expected to pay for, and if possible approximately what they will be expected to pay. This will avoid embarrassment on the night.

How you organise the collection of payments is up to you (or the organiser), and will depend on what the stag night involves. If you are going to a pub, and are thinking of setting up a kitty, remember that some people may drink much less than others and may resent having to pay more than their fair share. And whatever is involved, it would be wise for the organiser not to end up paying any large bill himself and then have to try to get the money back from the participants later on.

Most people will have enough money with them for the evening, or will be able to pay by cheque or plastic, but it would be a good idea if you had some extra cash with you in case of emergencies.

On an activities trip in the UK or on the continent, everyone, including the groom, should pay their own main expenses. But you will all probably want to buy the groom a drink at some point, and there may be some other way in which you can between you pay for something extra for him.

Stag party *dos, don'ts,* and things to remember

- Even if the groom knows where he is going and roughly what will happen, do try to get some unexpected element into the event. (And, please, *not* a kissogram girl! That is so yesterday. Be imaginative.)
- Give your stag party a theme, and dress accordingly. If not, how about getting special T-shirts printed for the occasion?
- You don't want to be a party-pooper, but your responsibility as best man is at all times to look after the groom. Do not let anyone force him to do anything he is not happy about. Do not let anyone do anything to him that he is not happy about. Do not let his friends buy more drinks for him than he can cope with. (Your job, by the way, is to remain sober enough to keep an eye on what is going on.) Do not let practical jokes get out of hand (no tattoos; no shaving off of his hair, etc; no stripping him naked and tying him to a lamp post; nothing too tasteless, and certainly nothing illegal or offensive to other people who may witness it). What might seem good fun after a few drinks may seem a lot less funny or clever the next morning. Nothing should be allowed that cannot be put right; nothing should be allowed that would upset the bride; nothing should be allowed that would spoil the wedding or the wedding photographs.

The local event

- If you are going to a restaurant, you would do well to book a private room so that you can enjoy yourselves without disturbing other diners.
- If you are booking entertainment of some sort, make sure that the entertainers know where to come, and when. Confirm the arrangements with the agency on the morning of the party. Give them your mobile phone number so that they can call you if they get lost or have to call off at the last minute, and if possible have a Plan B in case this happens.
- If organising food and drink, don't forget to cater for a variety of tastes: vegetarian food for non-meat-eaters, dairy-free food, nut-free food, etc. Does anyone have religious food requirements, such as kosher food? Some people don't drink alcohol, or may want low-alcohol drinks. Make sure there is enough food and drink for latecomers.
- Make transport arrangements before the event so that no one has to, or tries to, drive home while under the influence of drink. Have taxis organised, and have the numbers of local taxi companies with you. Don't let anyone who is not fit to drive get into a car: get them a taxi or get someone sober to take them home. Consider hiring a minibus or coach to take everyone home safely.
- If going to a club – especially abroad – be sure that you know exactly what you are paying for. Do not find yourselves the recipients of a large and unexpected bill at the end of the evening.
- If the groom does drink too much, don't let him near the bride or even contact her by phone or email. It is better that she doesn't know, and he may say or do something stupid.

The trip away

- If you are planning on going abroad, check well in advance that everyone has a valid passport (it is easy to forget such things in the anticipation of the event).

- If going on a weekend out of town or abroad, remind everyone about the travel arrangements and what to bring. Get everyone's mobile phone number, so that you can contact them on the day – especially if someone doesn't turn up on time – and make sure they have your mobile number too. Remind everyone to bring enough money with them for drinks, meals, and other expenses.

- If you are going abroad, make sure that everyone in the group has a written note of the name, address, and telephone number of the hotel you will be staying in. Then if anyone gets lost, they can ask for directions; or, if language is a problem – Tallinn and Prague are two very popular centres for stag events, but how many of your friends speak Estonian or Czech? And don't assume the locals will all speak some English – they can show the address to a taxi driver, look lost, and hope that the driver gets the point; or if they can find a public telephone, they can phone the hotel, where someone will no doubt speak English. It would also be sensible to have a note of the name, address, and telephone number of the local agent of the travel company you are booked with, if there is one.

- Far be it from this book to tell you how to behave on a stag party. If your and the groom's idea of a good holiday is to go to a Greek island ending in '*os*' and get drunk every night for a fortnight, you'll probably want to do much the same on the stag night or stag holiday. But remember that:

  (a) while many cities in the UK and abroad are geared up for stag weekends, there are still local laws and customs regarding acceptable and unacceptable behaviour; and while the police may be fairly tolerant, your behaviour must not stretch their tolerance to breaking point (and, in any case, you should have some consideration for the local residents);

  (b) if you and your friends turn up the worse for drink at an activity centre, you may not be allowed to take part in your planned activity;

  (c) if you and your friends turn up the worse for drink at a night-club or disco, you may not be allowed in;

    (d) if you and your friends turn up the worse for drink at an
        airport, you may not be allowed on your plane.
- Wherever you are going, a useful precaution would be to have the
  address and telephone number of the nearest British embassy or
  consulate, just in case you need help. But if you and your friends
  have been stupid, you can expect help from the embassy or
  consulate staff, but don't expect sympathy).

Whatever you do, make it an event to remember, an event that you
can remember, and, no less important, an event that you will want to
remember. And do be careful who sees the photographs!

The female best man and the stag party

If you are a female best man, what do you do with regard to a stag party?
Well, you have a couple of options, which you may need to discuss with
the groom:

- You could step aside and leave the lads to it, with someone else
  doing all the organisation. In that case, so that you don't miss out
  on a party, you might want to join the girls on the hen night
  instead.
- You could, on the other hand, suggest a joint stag and hen party.
  This will of course affect the choice of venue and activity, but it
  can still be very successful, if somewhat less riotous.

The groom's last night of freedom

Now that stag parties are not always held on the eve of the wedding,
some grooms like still to celebrate their 'last night of freedom' with a few
friends. This should be a much more restrained affair than a stag night,
with less drink flowing, followed by a (reasonably) early night.

The pre-wedding family party

Some families celebrate on the night before the wedding with a small dinner party for the bride and groom, their close families, and the best man and bridesmaid.

10 From 'three months to go' to 'D-Day minus one'

This is where things begin to hot up. During the three-month period before the wedding, there is a lot to be done. Some things will be mentioned in particular in this chapter, but you should be constantly consulting the wedding timetable to be sure that nothing is forgotten or left too late.

The groom

There are many things that the groom has to remember to do. You are his right-hand man, so make sure he has all he needs to have, and has done everything he needs to do. Has he covered all the legal requirements? If he is honeymooning abroad, is his passport up to date? Will he need inoculations, and when is he going to get them? Has he remembered to arrange foreign currency, etc.?

Has the groom got the ring, and does he know where it is? (Don't trust him on this – **get him to show you**. The morning of the wedding is not the time for him to discover that the ring isn't where he thought it was.)

Check travel timings

Check and double-check the time it will take from the groom's home/accommodation to the wedding venue. Do a couple of test runs, if possible at the same time of day and on the same day of the week as the wedding, so that you know how long it will take to get to the venue under the traffic conditions you can expect to encounter. Allow for predictable causes of delays and hold-ups on the wedding day, as well as for the unexpected. Is the local football team playing home or away that day? Is that the day of the monthly farmers' market? Might there be any parades or protest marches that you could get caught behind, or else roadworks and diversions? This information will tell you when you have to leave to reach the wedding venue on time. Put this time in your timetable. Also work out an alternative route in case traffic is unusually heavy or there is an accident blocking the road on the day.

If you will not be staying with the groom on the night before the wedding, you will also have to do a timing run from your house/accommodation to his, so that you know when to leave. You should also have a timing from the wedding venue to the reception venue.

Maps

Have maps prepared and sent out to guests, so they know their way around. The maps should show the wedding and reception venues and where cars are to be parked, if not at the venues themselves. They might also show some nearby hotels, restaurants, or pubs where guests could refresh themselves if they have come a long way.

It may be useful if the guests all have the chief usher's mobile phone number, so that they can contact him if they are really lost or late. (Not your number – you will be at the front of the church.) The phone must be switched off during the ceremony, though.

In case of more than expected delay in the bride's arrival, the bride's father can also phone the chief usher to let him know when she is likely to arrive.

The week before the wedding

Look through the timetable and checklists again to be sure that nothing has been missed, and finalise the wedding-day timetable for yourself and the groom. The wedding timetable on page 127 cannot give times for what is to be done on the day itself, as the actual times will depend on the distances involved, probable traffic conditions, and so on. **The timetable, therefore, is something you must work out for yourself.**

Once you have made your own timetable, give copies to the groom, the bride, and the ushers.

The hired cars

Check the arrangements a few days before the ceremony. You don't want to find that the bookings have been lost or the wrong date or time noted.

The day before the wedding

The suit

Collect your suit from the hire company and make sure that it fits. It is best to check this in the shop, not when you get home. Make sure that nothing has been forgotten.

Cars

If you are taking your own car to the church, check it is in working order. Check oil, water, and petrol, and give it a thorough clean inside and out.

If the groom's car is to be driven to the reception site this morning, agree with the groom how and when this is to be done, and make sure he has put his and the bride's honeymoon cases and going-away clothes in the boot.

The groom's wedding day needs

Has the groom got everything he needs? The ring, the marriage documents, his clothes, his speech.

Your wedding day needs

Gather the things that you need to take with you:

- your mobile phone
- money

- the notes or prompt cards for your speech
- the order-of-service sheets (if you have them)
- taxi firm phone numbers in case of emergencies
- spare handkerchiefs (you won't need them, but someone else might!)
- an umbrella (just in case)
- things to decorate the going-away car, and a cleaning kit.

Items for decorating the going-away car

If you are planning to decorate the couple's car before they leave, you will need suitable objects to tie on (such as the traditional old shoes, tin cans, cardboard horseshoes, balloons, and 'just married' signs, as well as string for attaching them, and some sort of foam, such as shaving cream, for writing on the car. (Make sure that whatever type of foam you choose will not damage the car's paintwork – if in doubt, try it out on a small corner of your own car first – and for the same reason don't use sticky tape.)

You should also make up an 'undecorating' kit (for example, a pair of scissors to cut the strings, some damp cloths and some dry dusters to wipe the car clean – quite simply, anything and everything the bride and groom will need in order to undo whatever it is you are planning to do to their car) and leave it in the car so that the decorations can easily be removed by the happy couple at some point after they have driven away.

The evening before the wedding

Get to bed early, and make sure the groom does. Set as many alarms as you need to ensure that you will get up on time the next day. If necessary, arrange a telephone alarm call, or ask a reliable friend to get you up at the right time.

11 The wedding rehearsal

If the wedding is to take place in a church or other religious building, it is normal to have a wedding rehearsal a few days before. A rehearsal may also be possible if the wedding is to take place in a hotel or restaurant, though that will depend upon the availability of the room for the rehearsal. It is not normal for there to be a rehearsal before a registry office wedding.

As best man, you must certainly attend the rehearsal. A wedding rehearsal is a good opportunity for everyone in the wedding party to get together (depending on the circumstances, it may be the first time that everyone has met in one place). In addition, the rehearsal is the time to check out exactly what will happen during the ceremony, ask necessary questions, make last-minute changes to arrangements, and iron out any problems that come to light.

It would also be a good idea at the end of the rehearsal, while everyone is there, to run through the whole wedding-day timetable. The rehearsal is also a good time to finalise arrangements for collecting buttonholes or order-of-service sheets, transport needed for guests, and so on. Going through everything at the rehearsal will be time well spent and may save you from some frantic moments on the day itself.

Correct etiquette for the wedding rehearsal

- Do not wear your wedding clothes to the rehearsal. Wear everyday but suitably respectable clothes.
- Turn up on time.
- Take the rehearsal, and the discussion and planning, seriously.

Be patient while matters that may seem trivial to you are thrashed out in excruciating detail.

- If you are in a church or other religious building, behave with appropriate reverence. You may not have strong religious feelings, but the minister and some of the wedding party will have. (That does not mean you have to be solemn and po-faced – you *can* laugh in a church.)

- It's all right for you to make suggestions, but remember that the minister already knows what has to be done and how it has to be done, and the bride and groom too will have their ideas of how things are to be done. (You may not like the music/hymns they have chosen but it certainly isn't your place to say so.)

Things to find out

If this is the first time you have been in the building, you and the ushers should check out:

- Where all the entrances and exits are (especially ones suitable for the disabled, if the main entrance/exit is not), and where the toilets are.

- Where the ushers should stand to greet the guests as they arrive.

- Lines of sight for the photographer, if there are to be photographs at the wedding, and/or for the video.

- Any possible obstructions to sight from certain seats – some old churches were not designed with wedding guests in mind and have pillars in awkward places – and therefore seats that ushers should not show guests into.

- The layout of the car park and where else guests can park.

Outline of the probable marriage ceremony

Most marriage ceremonies have the same basic structure. Obviously a formal church wedding may have more elements within that structure than a simpler registry office wedding, but the essentials will still be there.

The basic elements of a wedding ceremony are as follows:

- The groom and best man sit waiting for the bride to arrive.
- On being informed that she has, they stand and move to their positions for the ceremony, the best man to the right of the groom and usually slightly behind him. (The bride will come to the groom's left.) There will probably be a little time to wait at this point while photographs are taken of the bride and her father and the bridesmaid.
- The bride and her father walk down the aisle/passageway to where the groom, best man, and minister/registrar are waiting.
- The minister or registrar welcomes everyone and begins the ceremony.
- There may be readings, poems, prayers, and/or hymns. (Make sure you know the hymn tunes – it looks bad if the best man doesn't sing.)
- The minister or registrar asks if there is any reason why the couple should not be married.
- The minister or registrar marries the couple; the vows are made and the ring(s) given.
- There may be a musical interlude while the register is signed; you may be asked to be a witness.
- The wedding party proceeds back down the aisle/passageway and out of the marriage venue (where more photographs will be taken). The best man accompanies the bridesmaid (or the chief bridesmaid if there is more than one). The order of the procession is: bride and groom; chief bridesmaid and best man; other bridesmaids; bride's mother and groom's father; groom's mother and bride's father. (When escorting a lady you offer her your left arm.)

Different religious groups will have variations on this basic format. You will find these out at the rehearsal.

Double weddings

If two couples are getting married at the same service, each groom will have his own best man. Each best man has the same duties he would have if there was only one couple being married. In the service, one couple will go through the marriage vows first, then the other.

Things to check

As best man, your main responsibilities are to stand beside the groom and hand over the ring(s). You are not responsible for seeing the guests seated; that is the ushers' job. Usually the best man stays with the groom before the ceremony, but sometimes he is expected to wait at the door with the ushers to greet the guests until it is nearly time for the ceremony to start, when he then takes his place beside the groom. It is probably better that the best man be with the groom for the whole period of time before the ceremony, to keep him calm, but make sure at the rehearsal that everyone is in agreement about where you are expected to be.

Children

The rehearsal is a good time to get to know any little flower girls and pageboys that might be part of the wedding party. Make sure you know the children's names and which child belongs to which parents, so that you can call on appropriate help on the wedding day, or quickly return lost children to their parents.

By their behaviour at the rehearsal, you may also be able to size the children up and see whether you are likely to have problems with them on the day. Some will be more confident than others, and some more restless (if not downright bolshie – the little angels). They may suffer from nerves at the rehearsal or on the day and refuse to co-operate, or have a tantrum, or tears. The parents are there to deal with the major problems but you and the bridesmaid may have to take action quickly if someone starts demolishing the flowers or needs the toilet. None of the guests will mind – it will be one of the many 'Aaaaww' moments of the day.

Have a few suitable sweets in your pocket (at the rehearsal and on the day), but do check with the parents that it is safe to offer them to the children – there are so many food allergies around nowadays and you don't want a child to collapse from 'toffee poisoning' in the middle of the ceremony.

Music

If the ceremony is in church, the music may be provided by an organ or a band or both. The rehearsal is the time to ensure that the organist knows what to play, that there is room for the band, etc. If music is to be provided by CDs or the like, you should check that the venue has an adequate sound system for playing them, and you must know who is going to be responsible for actually playing the music at the appropriate times on the day.

Sometimes the couple ask a friend to play the organ in a church service rather than the church's own organist. Make sure that this has been cleared with the church's own organist beforehand – no one can play an organ if it is locked.

If there is no rehearsal . . .

If there is no wedding rehearsal, there are three things a best man should do:

- Go along to the marriage venue at some point before the wedding and familiarise yourself with the layout.
- Get together with all the 'main players' in the wedding ceremony sometime within the week before the wedding and make sure

that you are all quite clear and in agreement about what is going to happen and who is to do what when.

• If in any doubt about the form of the ceremony itself (e.g. when you have to produce the ring), check with the minister or registrar.

All the actions and questions that have been outlined above need to be dealt with whether or not there is an actual wedding rehearsal.

A dinner party after the rehearsal?

Sometimes the bride and groom arrange a small dinner or some other celebration for the wedding party after the rehearsal to thank everyone for their support. This is a suitable time to present the couple with your gift so that they can unwrap it at leisure. There is no need for a speech from the best man at such an occasion, though the fathers may well want to say something, but be prepared to stand up and say a few words about the bride and groom in case you are asked to do so. If no one else does so, you may want to propose a toast to the couple's future happiness, but that is all it needs to be, just an informal toast at a suitable moment:

> *I'm not going to make a speech this evening – it's quite enough that you should all have to suffer that on Saturday – but before we go home I'd just like to ask you all to join me in a toast to John and Julie's future happiness together. John and Julie . . .*

12 The wedding day: before the ceremony

Right, this is it, then. This is the day the bride and groom have been waiting for and that you have all been planning and preparing for – the high point of the 'marriage campaign' that you have been running.

You need to stay cool and calm. Keep your nerves under control, and help the groom do likewise. A best man who is running round like a headless chicken is no use to anyone. But there should be no need for that: you have prepared thoroughly for this day, you know exactly what is going to happen, you have your checklists and your wedding-day timetable, you have briefed the ushers, you have enough 'Plan Bs' to cover every emergency (check out the 'troubleshooting' panels), and your suitably short but excellent speech is safely in your pocket. All is well. Now, concentrate on the ceremony.

With regard to the ceremony, you have the two key tasks, and you already know what they are:

- Get the groom and yourself to the ceremony awake, sober, properly dressed, and on time.
- Have the ring safely on your person and be able to produce it at the right moment.

There is a third responsibility:

- Make sure the groom takes all the necessary paperwork to the wedding venue. If it is a church wedding requiring a marriage licence (called a 'certificate of marriage' in England and Wales and a 'marriage schedule' in Scotland and Northern Ireland), the minister actually has to see this before carrying out the ceremony – it is not enough that he or she should know that there is one.

You have gone through all the necessary checks and actions for the night before the wedding, so everything is under control. You're up and about and, so far, on schedule. What do you do next? Check the wedding timetable, and then work thorough the jobs in order.

- If you are with the groom, make sure he is up and about too. If you are not with him, phone to make sure he is awake. Then get yourself round there immediately – you want to keep an eye on him this morning, and it is easier to do that if you and he are in the same place. If for some reason that's not possible, phone him from time to time to check on his progress (but not to the point of driving him crazy with all your fussing!).
- Have a proper breakfast, and try to ensure that the groom has one too. Eating time should be in your timetable – it's important. If the wedding is in the early afternoon, you should have made arrangements for lunch as well – and if you won't have time for a proper lunch, at least arrange some sandwiches.
- Your timetable will allow you plenty of time to reach the groom's house if you are not already there, so set off promptly, taking your clothes and other essentials with you so you can dress at the groom's house.
- Confirm with the ushers the time they should be at the church, check they know their duties, and have their clothes and cars ready. Make sure the usher chosen for the job has the order-of-service sheets ready to take with him (unless you have them). Check that he or another usher is collecting the buttonholes and corsages from the bride, the florist, or the reception venue, if you are not doing this yourself.
- Phone to wish the bride and her parents well, and check there are

no last-minute problems you could help to sort out. This also gives you an opportunity to remind the bride's father to bring any cards, letters, etc. from well-wishers with him so that you have them with you at the reception. Remind him also to phone the chief usher on his mobile phone when he and the bride are setting off, and especially if they are delayed.

- If you are not in the same house as the groom's parents, phone them too, to wish them well and again make sure they don't forget the cards, letters, etc.
- Make a last check of the travel arrangements. If you're driving, make sure the car starts. Tie on the white ribbons. Check with a motoring organisation about possible roadworks, etc. If you are going by taxi or hired car, check again that they have the correct address and pick-up time.
- Once you and the groom are dressed, check that there are no price tags on your shoes, labels on your clothes, and so on.

Before you leave for the ceremony:

- Check that you and the groom have all the necessary marriage documents, honeymoon documents (honeymoon tickets, passports, etc.), the ring, and your speeches. Make sure you have money and your plastic with you in case of emergencies. Check the groom has his car keys if his car has been left at the reception venue.
- Take along any messages from well-wishers that have arrived at the groom's address.
- Just before you leave for the wedding venue, ask the groom to give you the ring. Place the ring safely in a pocket, not on your finger – it might slip off unnoticed or else you might not be able to get it off your finger at all during the ceremony.
- If there are fees to pay (see page 94), get the money from the groom. It is best if each fee is in a separate envelope, not as loose cash.
- Set off for the church promptly – if something goes wrong you will have time to handle it without upsetting the arrangements

for the ceremony. If you are going in your or the groom's car, *you* drive: the groom's mind may be too much on other matters for him to drive safely.

- Take an umbrella with you in the car, just in case.

Emails and text messages

People who are unable to attend the wedding may send cards, letters, or telemessages of congratulation, but in this computer age they may also send messages by email. You, the bride and groom, and their parents, assuming you all have email connections, should check on the morning of the wedding for any last-minute emails that need to be included at the end of your best man's speech.

Similarly, someone may send a text message. It would be a good idea if mobile phones could be switched on and checked at some point before the speeches start at the reception.

The quiet drink

It is not uncommon for the groom and the best man to go for a quiet drink before the wedding. (Just the one, mind!) You can do this before setting off from the groom's house (or wherever you are), or you could set off in good time (always a good plan in any case) and have a drink in a hotel or pub near the wedding venue. Sometimes the ushers join the groom and best man for a drink, then go off to attend to their duties while the groom and best man go along later. Whatever you do, do not drink too much, and do not be late for the ceremony. Remember also that some religious groups have very strong views about alcohol, and a pre-wedding drink may be frowned upon.

13 The wedding ceremony

You and the groom should arrive at the wedding venue at least fifteen minutes before the ceremony begins. (If you aim for thirty minutes, that leaves a margin for error.)

Check with the ushers that everything is in order, that they have the buttonholes and corsages and the order-of-service sheets. Remind the ushers to switch off their mobile phones (except the chief usher who should remain contactable until the wedding starts), and remind them to warn people not to throw confetti (if this is not permitted; it usually isn't these days).

Remember to switch off your mobile phone and make sure the groom does the same.

The ceremony

In a church, you and the groom will probably stay in the vestry (the minister's office) until about five minutes before the ceremony is due to begin, when you will go to your places at the front of the church and sit down. The groom may understandably be a little nervous while waiting, both in the vestry and in the church. Your job is to keep him calm and relaxed. Knowing the groom as you do, you will have to decide how best to do this. Some grooms will appreciate the distraction of some conversation; others may prefer to be left in peace to their own thoughts – which is fine, so long as their thoughts are not tending towards running away at the last minute! (See the Troubleshooting panel below.)

If the groom is nervous, his mouth may become dry, so it would be a wise precaution for him to take a glass of water into the church with him and put it at the front seat, where he can sip it before the service and from where, if necessary, you can pass it to him (as discreetly as possible) during the service. (It might not be a bad idea to have a glass of water at the front of the church on the bride's side too, for the same reason.)

When the bride arrives, everyone stands. You and the groom may turn briefly to smile a welcome to the bride as she walks down the aisle, and then move forward to stand in your places for the ceremony, you slightly behind and to the right of the groom. The bride will stop next to the groom, on his left, and her father will take a step back. The bridesmaid takes the bride's bouquet.

Some dos and don'ts for the ceremony

- Be as relaxed as possible, and try to keep your legs relaxed. Every few minutes, shift your weight from one leg to the other.
- Smile. But not *all* the time (you don't want to keep a fixed grin on your face for the whole ceremony).
- Do not put your hands in your pockets. Have them at your side, in front of you, or behind your back.
- Do not chew gum or eat sweets. However, it may be wise to have a cough lozenge or two with you in case you, the groom, the bride, or the bridesmaid starts coughing.
- Do not scratch yourself, clean your ears, or deal with any other bodily discomfort in an open and possibly unattractive way. Even if you are a bit nervous, don't bite your nails.
- Treat the ceremony seriously. It is not the place for practical jokes. *Don't* pretend to have lost the ring.
- If you have forgotten when the ring will be required, don't worry – just wait till you are asked for it.

Troubleshooting

This is the part of the marriage campaign which has the largest number of potential hiccups, so it is best to be prepared.

What if a hired car breaks down or gets lost?

You may need to use your own car, so make sure it is clean, filled with petrol, and in working order. In the event of your own car breaking down or not starting, you will need to quickly call for a friend to come and fetch you or for a local taxi to pick you up. In the first case, you should have arranged this in advance, so that the friend knows that he or she may be called on and is contactable by phone, in the second case, you should have a note of local taxi companies' phone numbers with you.

It is also possible that a wedding guest may phone up from somewhere needing transport. This is another reason to carry the phone numbers of local taxi firms with you, and you should make sure that the chief usher has a note of them too.

What if a guest gets lost?

If all the guests have been sent a map showing the wedding venue and the reception venue, there is no reason for anyone to get lost. But if they do – maps can easily be lost or left behind – they will need someone's mobile phone number as a contact number. You will be inside the building with the groom, so the best person to phone would be the chief usher. If it is OK with him, send out a note of his mobile number along with the maps (but on a separate piece of paper, not on the map, otherwise the telephone number gets lost along with the map).

What if the ring gets lost?

This should never happen if you follow the wedding timetable. Well before the day, you check with the groom that he knows where the ring is, and if he can't find it, there is still time to search for it. But *just in case* he can't find the ring on the day, you should have bought a cheap spare ring to use in its place. Have it on you when you go to fetch the groom to go to the ceremony. But if the real ring is not lost, make sure you produce the correct one at the ceremony!

What if the bride is *really* late?

There may be problems with her car, the driver may have got lost or gone to the wrong house, or there may be unforeseen traffic problems on the way to the wedding venue. Make sure there is an agreed plan for this eventuality. The bride and/or her father should have a mobile phone with them, and should phone you or the chief usher immediately the problem arises. And they should keep in contact until the problem is solved so that you know what their probable time of arrival at the ceremony will be. You may need to send a taxi for them, or else send one of the ushers in a car, so have that plan set up in your mind as well. You must let everyone know what has happened, and ask the organist (if there is one) to play a little more music.

What if the bride wants to call it off?

This is not directly your problem (the bridesmaid and the bride's parents will have to deal with it), but you will still be involved when the news has to be broken to the groom and his family. Again, your job is to be supportive and to keep the groom as calm as possible while the situation sorts itself out one way or another. The groom will probably want to see the bride, but this should only happen if the bride wants it and when she is ready for it.

What if the groom doesn't want to go through with it?

If this occurs at some point before the wedding day, there is time to deal with it. The groom will probably turn to you, his right-hand man, for advice; you have to listen and advise him as you see fit. Is it just nerves, or is there some real underlying problem?

Do *not* tell him that if he doesn't go through with the marriage, he will be letting everyone down. That will probably have occurred to him already. It won't help for him to be told so by you. It won't be the first time that a bride or a groom has feared, or realised, as the wedding day approaches that they are maybe making a mistake. Whatever he does next – go on or back out – he knows he might regret it. He needs time to think. So he needs support, not pressure. Your job is to give support and try as best you can to fend off the pressure.

What if the groom has realised he just doesn't want to marry the bride?

If it is not just a case of nerves, but the last-minute realisation that he really does not want to marry the bride, then the wedding will at least have to be delayed till the situation sorts itself out, and presumably called off altogether unless the groom changes his mind again. Obviously there will have to be talks with the groom's parents, and with the bride and her parents. If you are involved, as you should be, be careful not to take sides. Try to keep everyone calm and ensure the discussion is as unemotional as possible, and strictly to the point (nothing is achieved in a situation like this by people dragging up past hurts, grudges, and resentments).

What if it's a last minute panic?

This is much more of a problem. Decisions have to be made quickly, perhaps while the guests are actually arriving. Don't try to handle this yourself; call in the groom's father (or some other close relative) before you do the talking. Try to keep the groom (and everyone else) calm, and do not let the groom leave the premises. If the groom remains adamant that he does not want to go through with the ceremony, then you or someone will have to break the news to the bride and her father (who may be on their way to the ceremony, if they haven't actually arrived). You will have to decide whether it is your job to stay with the groom or to break the news to the bride. Whatever happens, do not phone the bride or her father – this is something that must be done face-to-face, and in privacy, where the bride can take in the news and express her emotions freely without embarrassment. The registrar or minister must of course also be informed as soon as possible, and the organist (if there is one), who may have to keep playing until a decision is made as to whether the marriage is to go ahead or not. If the ceremony is called off, it should be the bride's father who makes the announcement to the guests, as he is technically the host.

What if the bridegroom's gone AWOL?

It's your job to find him. (But why did you let him out of your sight in the first place?) Keep calm, and keep smiling. Move quickly, but don't rush around. There should be no fuss. First of all, tell the groom's parents and the registrar or minister what has happened, and again let the organist know that he will be playing for longer than expected, but if possible do not tell the bride or her family anything at this stage. Leave some of the ushers to look after the guests, but quietly gather the other ushers and a few other friends together out of sight of the guests and the bride's family, explain what has happened, and start looking for the groom. As best man, you must organise the search team, and send them out to the various places the groom might be. How long has he been gone? Where would he be likely to go? Back home? To the pub? He may not have gone far at all. Perhaps he is just wandering around in the churchyard or in nearby streets. Perhaps he is just hiding in the toilet. Look in the nearby places first, before working outwards in increasing circles. Don't forget your mobile phones – communication between the searchers will be crucial.

What to do when you find him

Be supportive, even though his reasons or fears may seem nonsense to you. He knows he is letting down the bride, both families, and all the guests, so he won't have taken the decision to run away lightly. If you can talk him round, and you are sure that this was just an attack of last-minute nerves and nothing more, then the ceremony can take place. Make up some excuse for the delay – say the groom wasn't feeling well and needed some fresh air. Don't tell the truth on this occasion. It's better that no one knows, unless the groom chooses to tell them. If, however, it is clear to you that the ceremony just cannot go on as planned, it will be up to you to go back and break the news to the bride and her family. You can expect tears, and do not be surprised if, as the bearer of bad news and the groom's close friend or relative, you bear the immediate brunt of their anger too. Don't argue back, just retreat and leave everyone to calm down. Whatever you do, do not at this stage tell the bride or her family where the groom is. The groom and bride will need to talk, but only after tempers have cooled and emotions have calmed. And having the bride's brothers coming round to sort the groom out will achieve nothing but a trip to a police station.

The marriage certificate

The completed and signed marriage certificate has to be taken back to the registrar within a certain number of days after the wedding has taken place (you or the groom should check this with the registrar), so you or some other person must attend to this if the bride and groom cannot. Whoever is to be responsible for this should be given the certificate immediately after it has been signed and **put it somewhere safe.**

A note on civil partnerships

A civil partnership ceremony will take place in front of a registrar. The form of the ceremony will be essentially the same as that for uniting a bride and groom in marriage at a registry office.

14 After the ceremony

The photographs

After the ceremony there will be more photographs, both the official ones and ones that guests and family want to take. You and the ushers may help the photographer gather the various groups together to be photographed. It will be useful, therefore, if you have a note of the various wedding groups the bride and groom want photographed.

Troubleshooting

What happens if the photographer doesn't turn up?
There are bound to be guests with cameras, but it would do no harm to find out in advance who among the guests might have a high-quality camera and, with luck, be an experienced photographer. Contact him/her before the day to ask if he/she would be willing to stand in *if* the photographer doesn't arrive. Make sure the chief usher knows where he can find him/her if there are to be photographs before the ceremony (when you will be inside with the groom) as well as afterwards.

It would also be useful to have an idea of what photographs are to be taken, so check in advance with the bride and groom (who should have discussed this with the photographer) and have the list with you so that you can help the substitute photographer take the photographs as speedily as possible. (See the checklist on page 139.)

Leaving for the reception

The bride and groom leave first, followed by the bridesmaid. Next the bride's parents leave, in their own car or a hired car, and then the groom's parents in their own car.

At more formal weddings, there may be additional official hired cars, one for the bride's mother and groom's father, the other for the bride's father and groom's mother.

When the wedding party has left, the other guests follow on to the reception. You will have organised any necessary lifts beforehand, but ask the chief usher to check that no one is left behind.

You may want to get to the reception venue promptly, and at least one usher should also go early to supervise the parking when the other guests arrive.

One or two ushers should check for anything left behind by the family or guests and take it to the reception.

Settlement of fees

For a church wedding, fees may be payable to the church, the minister, the church officer, caretaker or verger, the organist, a bell-ringer, and the choir. What fees are to be paid to whom should be checked in advance (perhaps at the rehearsal).

The best man may be asked to hand over the fees before or after the service, in which case the various fees should be in separate envelopes with the recipients' names on them. But it is surely better not to have to deal with this at all at the wedding; it is better if arrangements are made for the fees to be paid before or after the wedding day rather than on it. There are plenty of matters that have to be dealt with on the day, so if anything can be dealt with on another day, so much the better.

15 The reception and the speeches

The reception is usually held in a hotel or restaurant room hired for the occasion, or at the home of the bride's parents.

As best man, you should usually be among the first to arrive at the reception, along with the bride and groom, their parents, and the bridesmaid.

Receiving the guests

Most receptions have a receiving line, comprising the bride and groom, the bride's parents, and the groom's parents. You and the bridesmaid may also be asked to be in the line. If there is a master of ceremonies or toastmaster, he will announce the names of the guests as they arrive; if you are not in the line, you may be asked to fill this role. But at most weddings, the guests simply introduce themselves.

Guests are generally then offered a drink. There may be waiters and waitresses to do this, but otherwise it may be you and the bridesmaid (if you are not in the receiving line) and the ushers who see to this.

Wedding presents

It is not usual nowadays for there to be a showing of presents at the wedding reception, but some guests will probably arrive with their presents. Since the bride and groom can hardly shake hands and talk to people with their arms full of presents, there should be a table beside them on which they can place the presents as they get them, or else have an usher or two ready to take the presents and put them somewhere safe. (If you are in a hotel or restaurant, this will need to have been arranged with the management beforehand. There will also have to be arrangements made for taking the presents away after the reception.)

Well-wishers' cards and letters

When you have a moment, collect all the cards, letters, telemessages, etc. from people who cannot be at the wedding. You will already have any that have been sent to the groom, and you will have reminded the bride's and groom's parents to bring ones they have received. Remember that some messages may have been sent to the reception venue, so ask for these too.

Troubleshooting

What if either father has forgotten the cards and letters?
(But you *did* remind him in the morning, didn't you?)
If there is still time to fetch them, find out where they are and send someone for them. Otherwise, either ignore the problem and simply read the cards and letters you have (which may make one family wonder why great-aunt Jean in Australia didn't send a message), or admit that the cards have been left behind (which may embarrass the father concerned). Discuss with said father which he would prefer.

You should read over all the messages before the meal to make sure you can read the writing and decipher the signatures (ask a member of each family to help if you can't). You may want to note anything that is not suitable for reading out (i.e that is to be omitted when you read the messages), and decide how you will cut down messages that are very long (people sometimes include poetry or literary passages with their congratulations, but reading it all out might make the reading of the messages take longer than desirable – and sometimes the poetry is execrable anyway. The bride and groom and their families can read all the cards and letters again later on, including the bits you have missed out).

The meal

At an appropriate time, the toastmaster will ask the guests to take their seats. If there is no toastmaster, you could do this, or else the bride and groom may simply sit down at their table as a signal for the guests to take their seats.

At most weddings there is a top table for the wedding party. The seating arrangement is likely to be along the following lines (facing the guests):

Best man, groom's father, bride's mother, groom, bride, bride's father, groom's mother, bridesmaid.

Step-parents are usually also included, and the minister and his wife. If there is more than one bridesmaid, they may all be at the top table; alternatively, only the chief bridesmaid is at the top table, with the others seated elsewhere.

If a minister of religion is present, he should be invited to say grace. If there is no minister present, grace may be said by the bride's father, or by anyone else (including the best man, but why not pass that job on to someone else, especially if you are also acting as master of ceremonies?).

To introduce the person who will say grace, something along these lines is sufficient:

Ladies and gentlemen, before the meal begins I would like to invite . . . to say grace for us.

If you are saying the grace yourself, again something short and simple is best:

Lord God, on this happy occasion, we give you thanks for the food we are about to share and for the friends and family gathered here with whom we will share it. Amen.

You can get more ideas for graces from *Perfect Wedding Speeches and Toasts*, a companion volume to *Perfect Best Man*, or by googling on the Internet (for example 'grace+meal').

The speeches

After the meal come the speeches. The master of ceremonies (if there is one) or the best man (if there isn't) calls for silence and introduces the bride's father, who will propose a toast to the bride and groom.

The groom is then introduced, and replies to the toast on behalf of himself and his wife. He concludes his speech by proposing a toast to the bridesmaids.

The best man then replies to that toast on behalf of the bridesmaids. Your speech as best man is supposed to be one of the high points of the reception, but don't let that worry you, we'll deal with that in the next chapter. At the end of the speech, the best man reads out the well-wishers' messages.

If the bride has chosen to say something, she speaks next. The master of ceremonies should introduce her, or you should introduce her at the end of your speech.

Troubleshooting

- There are three main speakers at the reception: the bride's father, the groom, and you. You know you must remain sober enough to make your speech, but what to do if either of the other two get into a state that renders them almost speechless? Prevention should be your first objective – if you see that either of them is drinking more than is wise during the meal, have a word with them. If that doesn't work, you are going to have to have a Plan B. Who else could propose the toast to the bride and groom? Is there another family member who could step in? Don't wait until the last minute – approach them at once, because they are going to need time to get their thoughts in order. The groom's speech is more of a problem, as he obviously should reply to the toast to himself and his wife. Could the bride do it? If not, it's probably down to you as best man. Make light of the situation, give a brief apology and explanation (the situation will be pretty obvious in any case), and then get on with the speech, filling in briefly for the groom and then moving swiftly on to your own best man's speech, but including a toast to the bridesmaid somewhere along the way. (You might even raise a laugh if you thank yourself on behalf of the bridesmaid for your own toast.) If there is a master of ceremonies to introduce the speeches, make sure that he knows what is going on and who he should introduce.

- There is another way you, the bride's father, or the groom could find yourselves speechless. You've forgotten to bring your speech notes with you! Or they have been mislaid somewhere. The best thing is for each of the speakers to photocopy their notes and have the spare copies somewhere safe but accessible, for example in someone's car.

16 The best man's speech

This is the part of the day that many best men dread. It was all right being the organiser and campaign manager, but now the time has come for you to be the entertainment! But with the planning and preparation, you'll be fine. Remember that you've only got to fill about four minutes, and that after a good meal and a few drinks, everyone will be ready to be pleased by almost anything you say.

There are three things you need to know:

- how to prepare your speech
- what to put into the speech (and what not to!)
- how to deliver your speech.

We will deal with the 'what' first, and then the 'hows'.

Structure and contents of the best man's speech

The key elements of the best man's speech are:

- You thank the groom on behalf of the bridesmaid for his complimentary remarks and toast; if the groom has included flower girls and pageboys in his speech (as he should have), you include them in your thanks. Add your own compliments.
- If the bride and groom have given the bridesmaid, etc. gifts for their services, you say thank you for these as well. (You and the ushers will presumably also have had gifts, so include yourself and the ushers here.)

- Since the ushers have been your assistants throughout the day, you thank them for their help, with special mention of the chief usher, who has been your deputy.
- You might want to thank the caterers for their efficient service (if it has been – but if it hasn't, it's better to say nothing); if no one else has done so, you should thank the minister/registrar for their help (even if they are not present at the reception) and similarly the church caretaker, organist, etc. who have contributed to the success of the day. You may also have been asked by the bride or groom to make a special mention of someone or other they want to thank (though the bride's father or the groom could do this in their speeches).
- Add your own congratulations to the bride and groom; say something complimentary about the bride.
- Thank the groom for inviting you to be the best man; tell some (preferably embarrassing, but not too embarrassing) anecdotes about the groom, but also include some stories showing his good side.
- If necessary, you may at this point pass on any information the guests need regarding the rest of the evening's activities. This is, however, possibly better left until after your speech and the reading of well-wishers' messages. Sit down when you have finished speaking, and then, when the room has settled a bit, stand up again, get everyone's attention, and give out the information. If yours is not the last speech, wait until all the speeches are over.
- Read the cards, letters, etc. from well-wishers.
- Possibly, *just possibly*, you may propose a toast to someone (but *not* to the bride and groom. (See the 'Dos and don'ts' section below.)
- It may be you who then announces that the bride and groom will cut the wedding cake. (Alternatively, it will be the master of ceremonies if there is one.)

Dos and don'ts of the contents of the best man's speech

- Try to think of an opening line that will get people's attention and make them laugh. (*Not* 'Unaccustomed as I am to public speaking . . .', unless, for example, everyone knows you *are* accustomed to public speaking, in which case that line *might* just scrape a laugh.)

- Don't try to impress people or to seem cleverer than you are, or else you may come across as pompous or patronising. Just be yourself. Use everyday language.

- Don't put on a funny accent unless you are sure (a) that it will be considered amusing, and (b) that it won't offend anyone.

- Don't make fun of people unkindly. Yes, it's your job in the best man's speech to embarrass the groom about his past, but **don't go too far.** You're not out to ruin the groom's day or make the bride wish she had never married him. Do not mention any serious failings or failures. Do not mention anything the least bit dubious about the groom's past – it is certainly not the time for the bride and her family to learn something about the groom that the groom would not have wanted them to know. As best man, you are in a privileged position – don't abuse it.

- If you poke fun at the groom, do also mention some of his good points and his successes.

- Don't swear or blaspheme, and don't tell risqué jokes. If there's a chance that something might upset or offend anyone, don't say it. The golden rule is: if in doubt, leave it out.

- Don't mention the bride's or groom's past marriages or previous relationships.

- Don't make in-jokes. If you work with the groom, or were at university with him, or belong to the same sports club, etc., don't refer to people or events that other guests will know nothing about.

- Don't tell lies.

- **Do *not* propose a toast to the bride and groom at the end of your speech.** This has been done by the bride's father. You should, however, express your best wishes for their future together somewhere in your speech.

In fact, the best man does not propose a toast to *anyone* at the end of his speech, unless specifically asked to do so. For example, after reading the messages of congratulations and good wishes from people who are not at the wedding, you might, if the families want you to, propose a toast to 'absent friends'. Or you might be asked by the bride and groom to conclude your speech with a toast to their parents. (You should check in advance whether this, or anything similar, is wanted.)

Anecdotes

Your speech should include one or two anecdotes about the groom, and also about the bride if you know her well enough. You could, for example, talk about how you met the groom, how you came to be friends, how he behaved differently after he had met the bride, the moment you knew it was serious, etc. You could tell some behind-the-scenes stories about the wedding preparations or a story about something that happened during the stag party.

Jokes and quotations

Either you are good at telling jokes or you're not. If you're not, it might be a mistake simply to take a joke from a book or one that you have heard somewhere and parrot it in your speech, as you may not tell it well enough to be amusing. Nothing falls flatter than a badly told joke. As an alternative to a joke, you might use an interesting or amusing quotation, as quotations are easier to put across if you are not a natural joke-teller.

If you do tell a joke or use a quotation, you should try to integrate it into your speech. Don't just stop mid-flow, give the joke/quotation, and then go back to the speech again. In particular, if you are using a quotation, try to relate it to the bride and groom. For example:

- As Jane Austen famously said: '*It is a truth universally acknowledged, that a single man in possession of a good fortune, must be in want of a wife.*' Well, given how rarely John buys anyone a drink down the pub, he must have a real fortune by now, so Julie has chosen well.

- Jane Austen once said that '*Next to being married, a girl likes to be crossed in love a little now and again*'. But pity John if he ever crosses Julie – I've seen her kill flies at five paces with just a look.

- Groucho Marx once said that '*Marriage is a wonderful institution, but who wants to live in an institution?*' Well, people have often said that John should be put in an institution; perhaps we've found the right one for him at last.

- Someone once said that '*No woman should marry a teetotaller*'. Well, with John, Julie can certainly relax on *that* score.

Avoid using any quotation that implies that marriages are inevitably difficult or unhappy. This would be a good example of a quotation you should *not* use:

- 'Marriage is like life in this respect – that it is a field of battle, and not a bed of roses.'

Don't use very long quotations: they can be a bit boring, and your listeners may get lost in the middle somewhere. You can always miss parts out: it's a wedding speech, not a work of literature.

See below for comments about where to find jokes and quotations.

The messages from well-wishers

It is up to you to check that all the messages are appropriate for reading out in company that may include elderly people and children; for example, the message from the lads in the rugby club might have made them laugh, and might make you and the groom laugh, but might also offend some of the guests. Make a joke of it:

And finally, there is a message here from the lads in the rugby club that, since there are children present, I am not going to read out. If anyone wants to read what it says, see me afterwards.

How to write your speech

From the section above, you know what elements your speech should include. But before you can deliver a speech, you have to write it. (Do not, under any circumstances, try to deliver an off-the-cuff speech. Have it prepared. But don't be afraid to alter it and ad-lib as you go along. Something may have happened on the day, or been mentioned in one of the other speeches, that you will want to bring up again in yours.)

The best way is to get a notebook or open a computer file, and set out the structure of the speech you are to make under various headings:

- opening line
- thanks to groom on behalf of bridesmaid
- thanks to groom on behalf of self and ushers
- thanks to ushers
- thanks to other people?
- congratulations to bride and groom
- something complimentary about bride
- thanks to groom for invitation to be the best man
- anecdotes about the groom
- jokes that could be used
- quotations that could be used
- toast (if needed).

Collect ideas for each heading, and add them to your file. Note all the names you will want to mention. Ask the groom if there is anything special he intends to say about the bridesmaid, so that you can respond to it when you speak on her behalf.

If you cannot think of suitable anecdotes about the groom, ask mutual friends if they can remember any interesting or amusing episodes in his life.

You can get jokes and quotations from various sources:

- from the Quick Quotes on pages 120–4
- from books on wedding speeches (such as *Perfect Wedding Speeches and Toasts* and *Perfect Readings for Weddings*, companion volumes to *Perfect Best Man*)
- from joke books and books of quotations (look under 'wedding', 'marriage', 'bride', 'love', etc.)
- by asking friends if they know any suitable jokes and quotations (but do avoid the old chestnuts that everyone has heard before)
- by searching the Internet, for example under 'wedding jokes' and 'wedding quotations' (and you might get some good stories from a search for 'wedding disasters' too).

Another source of amusing quotations is in old books on marriage etiquette and household tips. You may find these in a library or a second-hand bookshop.

Once you have collected the material, and about two months or so before the wedding, you will need to put it into order, deciding what material to use and what to discard.

Make a first draft of the speech, then time yourself reading it out loud at the speed at which you will speak at the reception (which is slightly slower than normal speaking speed). Is the speech about long enough, too long, or too short? If it is too long, take something out; if it is too short, go back to your file and look for something to add.

Keep on drafting and refining your speech until you are satisfied that it is of the right length and flows smoothly from beginning to end.

At this point, you now have to decide what you will want to have in your hand when you make the speech. You could have the whole speech written out, or you could have a set of prompt cards with only the headings and main points on them to remind you of what you want to say. There are advantages and disadvantages to both.

If you have the whole speech written out, you will always have a note of what you want to say next. On the other hand, though, if you read your speech word by word from your notes, that can make the speech rather flat and boring. If you use prompt cards, you will probably speak in a more natural and lively tone, but there is always the possibility of you forgetting what you intended to say under a particular heading or key point, and your speech may become rather hesitant, with long pauses while you gather your thoughts for what you want to say next.

Whether you write out your speech or only have notes in front of you, it is best to use large file cards rather than paper, as cards do not flop or bend. Number the cards, so that if you drop them, you can quickly get them into the correct order again.

One solution is to have speech notes that combine both styles. Have the whole speech written out as a safety precaution, but have the headings and key points (such as the punchlines of jokes) in a different colour or in larger letters. (A computer is handy for this as you can use all sorts, sizes, and colours of font.) A line space between each line of writing is another good idea, as it makes your notes easier to read.

Once you have rehearsed your speech a few times, you will more or less know it off by heart in any case, and will only have to glance at your notes from time to time. But don't try to memorise your speech, as that too can make for a rather flat and uninteresting performance.

When rehearsing, watch yourself in a mirror or video yourself, so that you can see what you will look like to your audience. Many comedians and other performers do this. Decide how you are going to stand, and what you will do with your hands.

Practice makes perfect.

How to deliver your speech: some dos and don'ts

- You will doubtless have a drink or two during the reception, but never forget that you have to make a speech, so don't overdo it. If you think you *have* drunk too much, and you feel you may be a little unsteady of speech or unsteady on your feet, ask for a cup of coffee. It is also a good idea to have a glass of water beside you so that you can take a sip from time to time if your mouth dries up.

- There will always be some noise between speeches – people talking, laughing, coughing, moving their seats to get more comfortable, etc. So when you stand up to speak, don't try to talk over the noise, but give everyone a few moments to quieten down.

- Use the time while people are settling down again to get settled yourself. Move your chair back so you are not jammed against the table. Take a few deep breaths to relax, and get yourself into a relaxed, but upright stance (just like at the wedding ceremony, though you won't be on your feet for so long this time).

- Don't loosen your tie. Don't take your jacket off unless the room is very warm and others have done so (though they really should not have done even if they are feeling hot).

- Don't stand rigidly when you are speaking, but don't shuffle about either. You will be holding your notes in one hand, and perhaps a microphone in the other. But if you have one hand free, keep it under control: don't fiddle with the coins in your pocket or do anything else that would distract or annoy your listeners.

- Speak clearly and a little louder and slower than normal. Keep the tone conversational, as though you are talking to friends – which you are.

- Remember to breathe. That may sound obvious, but if you are nervous, you may tense up without realising it and not breathe properly, which will make your speech sound as tense as you are.

- Look around at the audience while you are speaking; don't just stare at your notes (but don't stare at any one person either or you will make them feel uncomfortable).

- Stick to the basic plan of your speech, but be flexible and don't be afraid to ad-lib if something occurs to you. If you do add new material, be brief, and don't waffle.

- Once it comes to reading the congratulatory messages, read them clearly and pause between each one, as people will probably be commenting on them to each other. Again, do not talk over the noise.

If there is a microphone, make sure you know how to operate it, and how to hold it – not too close to your mouth. Judge how loud you will have to speak – you won't have to speak as loudly as you would if you were speaking to the whole room without a mike.

What if there are two (or more) best men?

As has been suggested earlier on in the book, if there are two best men, one could make the best man's speech while the other could act as master of ceremonies at the reception and/or read out the letters and cards from well-wishers.

If both best men want to speak, however (for example, because you each know the best man in different contexts or from different periods of his life), the speeches need to be carefully thought out –and not too long. If you are speaking in turn, one way of arranging it would be as follows: the first speaker could cover the basic polite elements of the traditional best man's speech – thanks on behalf of the bridesmaid, thanks to the ushers on behalf of both best men, etc. – before contributing his anecdotes and jokes; he would then introduce the second best man, 'who would also like to say a few words about the groom'; the second speaker would then contribute his own anecdotes, etc. Be sure to check that you are not intending to tell very similar anecdotes or use the same jokes. When it comes to the reading of the cards and letters, either one or both of you could do it, in any way you have agreed on in advance.

If there are more than two best men (it's possible), the same applies as when there are only two. It's just a question of planning the speeches carefully and agreeing on who is going to say what.

If you have time and inclination, of course, you could write the best man's speech together, integrating each of your contributions into a single speech. At the reception you would stand up at the same time, whether or not beside each other, and bounce the speech back and forth from one to the other. If well rehearsed and well performed, this could be very entertaining.

17 After the speeches

You can begin to relax now. You've got through the wedding ceremony; you've given your speech. The worst is over.

The speeches are generally followed by the cutting of the cake, which may be served to the wedding party and guests then, or later on. Everyone begins to move around to chat to other people, and the dancing may start soon. (All this will have been decided beforehand, so you will know what the evening timetable is.) When people are chatting together, watch that there is no one sitting on their own, and if there is, go and talk to them, and introduce them to some of the other guests.

The evening reception

It's time to party! But your duties as best man aren't over yet.

When it comes to the first dance (probably a slow waltz), the bride and groom will start the dancing, followed by the best man and the bridesmaid, then the bride's and groom's parents, and finally by all the families and friends. After that, you should dance at least once with the bride, the bride's mother, and the groom's mother, and of course stepmothers if there are any, and if possible with some of the female guests, especially any ladies who are on their own. (You *did* take those dancing lessons, didn't you?)

If your wife, fiancée, or girlfriend is at the reception, you will obviously want to spend much of the evening with her, but nevertheless it is your responsibility as best man to make sure no female guest is left on her own while the dancing is going on – ushers and other male friends can be asked to help out with this. (You should, of course, also make sure that no *male* guests are left out either. Everyone must have a good time, and it is up to you, as far as possible, to see that they do.)

Troubleshooting

What if the band or DJ fails to show up, or their equipment doesn't work?

You will need an alternative source of music. It would be handy to know in advance if anyone can play the piano (and if there is a piano available at the reception venue). But you probably don't want to rely on an impromptu pianist for the whole evening, so you should also have a CD player, and a selection of suitable CDs in the boot of your car just in case. If you haven't got a suitable CD player, borrow one.

What if anyone gets too drunk or if an argument starts?

Take immediate action to control and calm the situation by getting the troublemaker(s) away from everyone else and/or each other. You may need help. But be prepared – you should before the day have found out about such possible tricky situations, and planned who to ask for help. Better still, keep a watch on things (especially the likely suspects you have been warned about) and try to step in before the problem even starts.

If the bride and groom are going to use their own car, you should keep a careful eye on how much they are drinking.

You don't want to spoil the party but you should try to ensure that guests do not keep on buying the groom celebratory drink after celebratory drink. (You need to watch your own intake of alcohol throughout the evening, so that you can guard the groom, as is your responsibility.) In fact, since the bride and groom are almost bound to have a few drinks during the evening, there is a high chance they will be over the limit, so for safety's sake it would be better to have planned for them to use a taxi or chauffeured car in any case.

What if there is a sudden need for a car and a driver at some point in the evening?

Unexpected emergencies happen. It would be handy to know the names of a couple of guests at the reception who can drive but will not be drinking.

What if a guest, deliberately or accidentally, damages property at the reception?

Although clearly, as best man, you will want to step in as quickly as possible to minimise any damage, you may not be able to prevent it. Financially, it is not your problem; you cannot be held responsible for what someone else does, and you are not the host of the occasion. If a guest causes damage to property at the reception venue, that is an issue either between the guest and the venue management, or between the guest, the father of the bride, and the venue management. The same applies if the damage is to the property of anyone attending the reception.

Your job, if you need to get involved, is to keep everyone calm and prevent fights. If there is an argument, and you can't stop it, try at least to get those involved not to argue in public. Get them out of the room, go with them (preferably with a couple of others you can trust to help you), and stay with them until tempers calm. If possible, persuade all involved to let the matter lie until after the reception is over, so as not to cause any further upset.

Decorating the going-away car

If the bride and groom's going-away car is going to be decorated, it is usually the best man who sees to this, even if others are doing the actual decorating. There are various things to remember:

- If the going-away car is a hire car, the car-hire firm's permission must have been obtained before even so much as one cardboard horseshoe is tied on.
- Nothing must be done to a car that would damage it or that might make it unsafe to drive, so keep a sharp eye on what the others are doing and put an immediate stop to any ill-advised activity. Mirrors and windscreens must be kept clean and clear of obstructions or distractions.
- You should remember to pack in the back of the car or in the boot the cleaning kit that you made up, so that the bride and groom can stop after a short drive and clean up the car if they want to.

The going-away

After the reception, the bride and groom will probably leave for their honeymoon.

If they are leaving by taxi, you should make sure they are ready in good time. If they seem to be unaware of time passing, remind them when they should go to change their clothes to be ready to leave. You and the bridesmaid should help the couple carry their luggage to the taxi. If the couple are going in their own car, bring it to the front of the venue and see that all their luggage is packed in it.

Make sure:

- that you get the groom's wedding outfit from him before he leaves, as you will be taking it back to the hire company for him;

and between you and the bridesmaid check:

- that nothing has been left in the bride's and groom's rooms by mistake, and that the couple has all necessary tickets and travel documents for the honeymoon;
- that the bride has her bouquet ready for her traditional parting gesture of throwing it over her shoulder to the crowd.

You or the bride's father should announce to the wedding guests that the couple is about to leave, so that everyone has time to cluster round the door to say goodbye.

The end of the evening

The party will probably begin to break up once the bride and groom have left. You are still on duty.

Along with the bride's and groom's parents, you should see the guests safely away. If a coach has been hired to bring guests to the reception, then a time will also have been arranged for it to take the guests back home again, or to where their cars are parked (presumably near the wedding venue). Make sure that all the guests know when the coach is due, and **check that all the guests who should be on it *are* on it before it leaves.** (You don't want someone emerging from the toilet to find that their transport home is already two miles down the road.)

Make sure that the bride's parents collect any presents that guests have brought to the reception, the remains of the cake, and the bride's dress. You already have the groom's suit.

Wherever the reception is being held, the caterers should deal with any clearing-up, but if there is anything that needs to be done by the family, make sure you offer to help. At any rate, you should have a quick look round to see that nothing has been left behind by the wedding party or the guests.

And now, at last, you can relax. Your duties are over.

An alternative scenario

Very often nowadays, if the reception is being held in a hotel, the wedding party (including the bride and groom) and some or all of the guests stay in the hotel overnight, even if some of them do live close enough to the hotel to go back home after the reception. There is a lot to be said for this, as (among other things) it avoids any issues over drinking and driving.

If the newlyweds or anyone else has to make a prompt start the next day, it would be wise to leave the early morning calls to the hotel staff (who will not sleep in) rather than to a member of the family or one of the guests (who may do). You should make sure that everyone who needs an early call has informed the hotel reception.

Whether the newlyweds join everyone else for breakfast is up to them, but you should make sure that all the family and guests know when they will be leaving the hotel so that everyone can be there to wish them well as they go. To avoid any disappointments, make sure everyone is at the front of the hotel in good time; check no one is missing.

Who pays for the best man's overnight stay?

There is no definite answer to this question. Given the wedding expenses that others will have to bear, if you can afford to pay for your own accommodation, it would be thoughtful to do so, or at least to offer (your offer may be turned down if the bridegroom or the bride's father considers it to be his responsibility). If, however, paying for an overnight stay at a hotel well beyond your normal price range is going to cause you financial difficulties, you will simply have to raise the matter with the bridegroom at a suitable point. There is no absolute necessity for you to stay in the hotel so long as you carry out all your necessary tasks or deputise someone else to do them on your behalf, and perhaps a member of the family or a friend who lives nearby could offer to put you up for the night without it becoming obvious that you can't afford to stay in the hotel. It's a slightly tricky and potentially embarrassing situation, but remember that you may not be the only one facing this problem: if you admit that staying in the hotel would cause you financial difficulties, you may make it easier for others to admit to the same problem.

18 After the wedding

There aren't many things for the best man to do after the wedding day, but they are all important:

- You should take your wedding outfit and the groom's back to the hire company.
- You should take the marriage certificate to the registrar, or check that the person responsible for doing so has not forgotten.
- If the bride and groom have given you a gift for being the best man, you should write and thank them for it straightaway, even though they are on their honeymoon.
- You should write to all the ushers to thank them for being your assistants throughout the day.
- You should write to the bride's parents to thank them for hosting the reception.

To ensure a perfect end to the honeymoon, if someone has a key take some flowers and perhaps some essential food items (such as fresh bread and milk) round to the couple's house the day before they get back. And how about a bottle of champagne to welcome them home?

Celebration party

If the bride and groom hold a celebration party when they get home, it probably isn't an occasion for speeches. You've been there and done that. But a short toast to their future health and happiness would be quite in order, and as best man, it is quite right that you should be the one to propose it.

Something quite simple is all that is needed: you are pleased to see the bride and groom back, glad they enjoyed their honeymoon, and would just like to ask everyone to join with you in wishing them all the best for their future together. Then enjoy the party.

Quick quotes

In this Quick Quotes section, you will find a selection of interesting and amusing quotations. Have a look through it and you might find the very one you need for your speech.

Some of the people quoted are well-known names, others are not at all well known but are included here because the quotation seemed apt. For well-known names, you could say in your speech, for example: 'As Robert Burns wrote in one of his poems, . . .', while for people your audience are unlikely ever to have heard of, you might be better to say: 'As someone once said, . . .' or 'As an American writer once put it, . . .', etc.

All you need is love.
Beatles' song title

Love means never having to say you're sorry.
Love Story film script

Real love is a pilgrimage.
Anita Brookner, English writer

Love is the wisdom of the fool and the folly of the wise.
Samuel Johnson, English writer

Marriage has many pains, but celibacy has no pleasures.
Samuel Johnson

Love conquers all things except poverty and toothache.
Mae West, American actress

Love is like a precious plant. You can't just accept it and leave it in the cupboard or just think it's going to get on by itself. You've got to keep watering it. You've got to really look after it and nurture it.
John Lennon, English singer-songwriter

Love is insanity.
Marilyn French, American author

Love does not consist in gazing at each other but in looking outward together in the same direction.
Antoine de Saint-Exupéry, French writer

Come live with me, and be my love,/And we will all the pleasures prove.
Christopher Marlowe, English poet

Love is an act of endless forgiveness, a tender look which becomes a habit.
Peter Ustinov, British actor

A man has only one escape from his old self: to see a different self – in the mirror of some woman's eyes.
Clare Boothe Luce, American writer

For a marriage to have any chance, every day at least six things should go unsaid.
Jill Craigie, British writer

No woman ever falls in love with a man unless she has a better opinion of him than he deserves.
E.W. Howe, American writer

Love and marriage, love and marriage/Go together like a horse and carriage.
Sammy Cahn, American songwriter

Marriage is popular because it combines the maximum of temptation with the maximum of opportunity.
George Bernard Shaw, Irish playwright

Like fingerprints, all marriages are different.
George Bernard Shaw

Husbands are like fires. They go out when unattended.
Zsa Zsa Gabor, Hungarian–American actress

A man in love is incomplete until he has married – then he's finished.
Zsa Zsa Gabor

A successful marriage is an edifice that must be rebuilt every day.
Andre Maurois, French author

Chains do not hold a marriage together. It is threads, hundreds of tiny threads which sew people together through the years. That is what makes a marriage last – more than passion or even sex!
Simone Signoret, French actress

Marriage is one long conversation, chequered by disputes.
Robert Louis Stevenson, Scottish writer

All any woman asks of her husband is that he love her and obey all her commandments.
John Raper, American writer

To keep your marriage brimming,/With love in the loving cup,/Whenever you're wrong, admit it;/ Whenever you're right, shut up.
American poet Ogden Nash's advice to husbands

One should not think too much about it when marrying or taking pills.
Dutch proverb

A good marriage is one which allows for change and growth in the individuals and in the way they express their love.
Pearl Buck, American author

A happy marriage is still the greatest treasure within the gift of fortune.
Eden Phillpotts, English writer

Marriage is not all bed and breakfast.
R Coulson

A man's friend likes him but leaves him as he is: his wife loves him and is always trying to turn him into somebody else.
G. K. Chesterton, English writer

But to see her was to love her,/Love but her, and love for ever.
Robert Burns, Scottish poet

Being a husband is a whole-time job.
Arnold Bennett, English writer

Love is composed of a single soul inhabiting two bodies.
Aristotle, Greek philosopher

A successful marriage requires falling in love many times, always with the same person.
Mignon McLaughlin, American writer

Two souls with but a single thought,/Two hearts that beat as one.
Baron von Munch-Bellinghausen, Austrian dramatist

Let the wife make the husband glad to come home, and let him make her sorry to see him leave.
Martin Luther, German priest

Marriages are made in heaven and consummated on earth.
John Lyly, English playwright

In every marriage more than a week old, there are grounds for divorce. The trick is to find, and continue to find, grounds for marriage.
Robert Anderson, American economist

Quick reference 1
The main duties of the best man and the ushers

The best man's main duties:

Be the bridegroom's assistant, confidant, and troubleshooter.

Be the wedding campaign manager.

Help in any way necessary with the wedding planning and preparations.

Organise the stag party, or ensure that it is organised by someone.

Get the groom to the wedding venue on time and in a fit state to go through with the ceremony.

Supervise the ushers.

Have the wedding ring, and produce it when required during the ceremony.

Help the photographer organise people for the wedding photographs (if necessary).

Ensure that everyone has transport and directions from the wedding venue to the reception venue.

Act as master of ceremonies at the reception, unless someone else is doing this.

Make a speech at the reception, and read out well-wishers' cards, letters, etc.

When necessary, act as escort to the (chief) bridesmaid.

Help guests to enjoy the reception, if necessary serving drinks to other guests.

The ushers' main duties:

Be the best man's assistants.

Hand out the buttonholes to the members of the wedding party (if necessary).

Help organise the parking of the guests' cars at the wedding venue and the reception venue.

Assist with the seating of guests at the wedding venue, and hand out the order-of-service sheets.

Help the best man organise people for the wedding photographs (if necessary).

Help the best man ensure that everyone has transport and directions from the wedding venue to the reception venue.

Check the wedding venue for anything that guests may have left behind.

If necessary, act as escorts to bridesmaids.

Help guests enjoy the reception, if necessary serving drinks to other guests.

Quick reference 2
The wedding timetable

Twelve months to six months before the wedding

Put the date and time of the wedding (if known) in your diary.

If the date and time of the wedding are not yet decided, get a decision soon.

Rearrange any prior commitments.

If possible, meet the whole wedding party. Failing that, if they do not already know you, write to them to introduce yourself.

Buy an engagement present.

Have a planning meeting with the bride, the groom, and the bridesmaid. If that is not possible, get in touch (and keep in touch) by phone and/or email.

Investigate possible reception venues, and check out prices, menus, facilities, the number of people they can cater for, car parking, master of ceremonies, etc.

Investigate prices and available car selection of local car-hire companies.

Investigate prices and available clothes selection of local dress-hire companies.

Have as many planning meetings as are required, as often as required.

Open a file of the contact details of all the main wedding participants and officials and the times of the various events (see the checklists, page 134).

Begin to plan the stag party.

Begin to plan your speech.

Six months to three months before the wedding

Continue to review the wedding and reception plans and firm up as many details as possible. The wedding venue, the reception venue, and the reception entertainment/band should have been booked by now.

Book whatever wedding-day transport is needed.

Firm up the details of the stag party, invite the guests, and make bookings if travel and activity events are involved.

Check that the ushers have noted the date and time of the wedding in their diaries.

You and the groom should get fitted for your wedding suits. If the ushers are not with you, give them the details of the dress-hire company, and check that they are arranging their own outfits in good time.

Continue to note down ideas for your speech.

Start to fill in gaps in your knowledge about the families and guests, especially family politics and potential minefields. Compile a list of close family, and ask to see family photographs, so that you recognise guests on the day.

Start dancing lessons if you need them.

Three months to two months before the wedding

Check again that the groom has dealt with, or is remembering to deal with, all the legal formalities for the marriage (the local registrar or the minister will advise) and any admin, bookings, health matters, etc. required for the honeymoon (a travel agent will advise).

Finalise the plans for the stag party (if it does not involve travel or specially organised activities), invite the guests, and book a room, entertainment, etc. if necessary.

Consult the wedding gift list (if there is one) and buy your present for the bride and groom.

Two months to one month before the wedding

Visit the reception venue with the bride and groom to check again on the arrangements.

Check that the wedding invitations and the order-of-service sheets are being printed, and when they will be ready for collection.

Contact the wedding planner, if there is one, and check on their plans for the wedding.

Begin to draft your speech.

One month to one week before the wedding

Carry out route planning and timings.

Check that the buttonholes and corsages (see checklist, page 138) have been ordered.

Check the groom has the ring and knows where it is.

If you will be using it on the day, have your car serviced; check the groom's car has been serviced if he will be using it.

Prepare maps for the guests and send them out.

Finish your speech, practise it and time it. Write prompt cards if you want them and practise the speech using them.

Have a word with the photographer about arrangements at the wedding and the reception.

Get your hair cut.

Buy ribbons for the wedding cars, unless they are coming with the cars. Buy decorations for the couple's going-away car if you plan on decorating it.

For a local stag night, check bookings and transport arrangements.

The final week

Attend the wedding rehearsal if there is one.

Finalise the wedding-day timetable and copy it to the groom, the ushers, and the bride.

Check the ushers know their duties; tell them or remind them of any special arrangements (disabled people, etc.).

Check all car-hire arrangements to see that everything is in order.

Check parking arrangements at the two venues again.

Give your gift to the bride and groom at a suitable moment.

Collect the order-of-service sheets from the printer, or see that someone does.

The day before the wedding

Collect your hired suit, and check everything is there and fits correctly.

Check with the florist that the buttonholes and corsages are ready and whether they are to be collected or delivered.

Collect the order-of-service sheets from whoever has them (unless you have arranged for an usher to do so).

Clean and check your car; fill it up with petrol.

If the groom is using his car to leave after the reception, make sure it has been checked and filled up, and parked at the reception venue. The couple's going-away luggage can be locked in the boot or, perhaps better, it can be taken into the reception venue to be stored safely. If you are going to decorate the car, pack a cleaning-up kit in the car.

Make sure you have plenty of cash in case of emergencies.

Charge up your mobile phone.

Check that the bride and groom (or someone from their families) will bring any cards, letters, etc. they have received for you to read out at the reception.

Gather all your wedding-day essentials together.

The evening before the wedding

Read over the wedding-day timetable again.

Check your clothes, iron anything that needs ironing, hang the clothes up, and polish your shoes. Check that the groom does the same.

Set your alarm clock(s); arrange an alarm call if necessary.

The wedding day

Before the ceremony
Wake up and get up.

Wake the groom, and see that he is up.

Have breakfast, or (better) go to where the groom is and have breakfast with him.

Phone the ushers, the bride or bride's parents, and the groom's parents and check that everything is under control. Where are the buttonholes and corsages, and the order-of-service sheets? Is there any last-minute problem, or does anyone need help? Remember the cards, letters, etc from well-wishers.

Make a last check of the travel arrangements.

Have lunch (if it's an afternoon ceremony).

Make sure you have the paperwork, the ring, the speeches, money, and the honeymoon documents (passports, tickets, etc.). Leave on time for the ceremony, or earlier if going for a drink first.

Arrive at the church or registry office at least fifteen minutes before the ceremony.

Check with the ushers that everything is in order. Remind them to switch off their mobiles (except the chief usher), switch yours off, and check the groom does the same. Remind ushers to stop people throwing confetti.

You and the groom take your places about five minutes before the ceremony is due to start.

After the ceremony

Help the photographer to sort out guests for photographs.

Remind ushers to check for property left behind, and to make sure all guests have transport to the reception.

Pay fees (if necessary).

At the reception

Give the master of ceremonies the names of the speakers.

Check you have the cards, etc, and find time to read them over before you make your speech.

Decorate the going-away car.

If necessary, remind the bride and groom when it is time to leave.

Tell guests when the couple are leaving.

Collect the groom's suit to take back to the hire company.

Help if necessary with clearing-up.

Check round the reception venue for anything that may have been left behind.

Final duties

Return suits to the hire company.

Take the marriage certificate to the registrar, or see that someone does.

Write thank-you letters to the couple for their present, to the ushers for being your assistants, and to the bride's parents for hosting the reception.

Quick reference 3
Checklists: people, places, times, and requirements

Create these files in a notebook.

1. The ceremony and the reception

You need the
    name
    address
    telephone number (day and evening)
    mobile number (if they have one)
    email address (if they have one)

of the following people:
    groom
    bride
    groom's father
    groom's mother
    bride's father
    bride's mother
    bridesmaid/matron of honour (or chief bridesmaid if there is to be more than one)
    other bridesmaids (if more than one)
    flower girls/pageboys (contact details for their parents; note the children's ages as well)
    usher/chief usher
    other ushers (if any)

In addition, you need full details of . . .

    the wedding venue
    vicar/minister/priest/rabbi/registrar
    verger/church officer/caretaker
    organist?
    bell-ringer?
    choir master?

    the wedding planner?

    the photographer

    the florist

    the printer

    the outfitter/clothes hire company
    contact
    date for collection of outfit
    date for return of outfit

    the reception venue
    contact
    provider of music (if any)

    the car hire company
    car/s to be supplied
    date/time for collection/delivery/pick-up
    the local taxi company/-ies

2. Planning and preparation

Planning meeting 1
    date:
    place:
    time:

Planning meeting 2
    date:
    place:
    time:

Planning meeting 3
    date:
    place:
    time:

Planning meeting 4
    date:
    place:
    time:

Wedding rehearsal
    date:
    time:

3. The stag party

Depending on what is being organised, you may need full details of
    the venue/-s
    contact/-s
    place/-s
    time/-s (room or table booked from . . .)

    local taxi company/-ies
    taxis booked at . . . to collect guests from (restaurant/pub)

    travel agent or other organiser (if any)
    contact

    all those taking part in the stag party/-ies
    especially phone/mobile phone numbers

4. Other parties

Engagement party (or other get-together)
  date:
  place:
  time:

Pre-wedding/rehearsal meal
  date:
  place:
  time:

'Final night of freedom' party
  place:
  time:

5. Transport requirements

To the ceremony
  Car for bridesmaid and bride's mother?
  Car for bride and father?

  Car for groom and best man? Whose? Hired? Taxi?

  Other cars required:

To the reception
  Car for bride and groom?
  Car for bridesmaid?
  Car for bride's parents?

  Best man?
  Ushers?

  Other cars required:

Lifts for guests required:

Cars with spaces in them:

Coach?
If so, who is travelling on it?

From the reception

Car for bride and groom? Their own? Taxi?

Other transport needs:
Coach?
If so, who is travelling on it?

6. Buttonholes and corsages

Buttonholes
groom
(male) best man
bride's father
groom's father
ushers
others?

Corsages
bride's mother
groom's mother
(female) best man
others?

7. Photographs to be taken

Discuss the actual requirements with the bride and groom and/or the photographer, but they are likely to include:

before the ceremony
> bride and father
> bride and bridesmaid/-s

after the ceremony
> bride and groom
> bride, groom, best man, and bridesmaid/-s
> bride, groom, and both sets of parents
> bride and groom and bride's parents
> bride and groom and groom's parents
> bride and bridesmaid/-s
> groom and best man
> groom, best man, and ushers
> bride and groom and bride's family
> bride and groom and groom's family
> (bride and groom and) all the guests

at the reception
> cutting the cake

Quick reference 4
Further sources of advice and information

The following lists provide a selection of other books and some websites where you may find further useful information about being a best man and about making the best man's speech.

Some of the books may be available in libraries as well as in book shops. And there are of course many wedding-related websites, which can be found by searching online.

For being a best man and giving a speech

Bowden, J *Making the Best Man's Speech* Oxford: How To Books, 2000

Davidson, G *Perfect Wedding Speeches and Toasts* London: Random House, 2007

Hobson, C *The Best Man's Organiser* Slough: Foulsham, 1997

Lansbury, A *How to Be the Best Man* London: Cassell Illustrated, 1994

Law, J *Perfect Readings for Weddings* London: Random House, 2007

Sources of jokes and quotations

Bloomsbury Dictionary of Quotations London: Bloomsbury Publishing, 1992

Chambers Dictionary of Modern Quotations Edinburgh: Chambers, 1993

Murray, M Mitch *Murray's One-Liners for Weddings* Slough: Foulsham, 1994

The New Penguin Dictionary of Quotations London: Penguin, 2006

The New Penguin Dictionary of Modern Quotations London: Penguin, 2003

The New Penguin Dictionary of Modern Humorous Quotations London: Penguin, 2002

The Oxford Dictionary of Quotations Oxford: Oxford University Press, 2004

www.aarons-jokes.com
www.ahajokes.com
www.hitched.co.uk/jokes
www.matrimonialbank.com/jokes

(There are many other websites where you will find marriage-related jokes and quotations, though many of them seem simply to copy from each other and their material is often very similar. Do a search for 'wedding jokes', 'marriage jokes', '+wedding +jokes' '+best man +jokes', etc. Some of the jokes are suitable for the wedding speech; others, you will find, are suitable only for the stag party!)

Perfect Wedding Speeches and Toasts

George Davidson

All you need to give a brilliant speech

- Have you been asked to 'say a few words' on the big day
  and don't quite know how to go about it?
- Do you want easy-to-follow tips on making a speech
  that is both meaningful and memorable?
- Do you want some guidance on how to improve
  your skills as a public speaker?

Perfect Wedding Speeches and Toasts is an invaluable guide to preparing
and delivering unforgettable speeches. Covering everything from
advice on mastering your nerves to tips about how to make a real
impact, it walks you through every aspect of preparing for the big day
and speaking in public. Whether you're the father of the bride, the
bride herself, or the best man, *Perfect Wedding Speeches and Toasts* will
help make sure your speech goes off without a hitch.

The *Perfect* series is a range of practical guides that give clear and straightforward advice on everything from getting your first job to choosing your
baby's name. Written by experienced authors offering tried-and-tested
tips, each book contains all you need to get it right first time.

BOOKS

Perfect Readings for Weddings

Jonathan Law

All you need to make your special day perfect

- Do you want your wedding to be that little bit more special?
- Do you want to personalise the ceremony by including readings that are just right for you?
- Do you need help tracking down a traditional reading, or finding something more out of the way?

Perfect Readings for Weddings is an anthology of the best poems, prose passages and quotations about love and marriage. Including everything from familiar blessings and verses to more unusual choices, it covers every sort of reading you could wish for. With advice on how to choose readings that complement one another and tips on how to ensure that everything runs smoothly on the day, *Perfect Readings for Weddings* has everything you need to make sure the whole ceremony is both memorable and meaningful.

BOOKS

Perfect Babies' Names

Rosalind Fergusson

All you need to choose the ideal name

- Do you want help finding the perfect name?
- Are you unsure whether to go for something traditional or something more unusual?
- Do you want to know a bit more about the names you are considering?

Perfect Babies' Names is an essential resource for all parents-to-be. Taking a close look at over 3,000 names, it not only tells you each name's meaning and history, it also tells you which famous people have shared it over the years and how popular – or unpopular – it is now. With tips on how to make a shortlist and advice for avoiding unfortunate nicknames, *Perfect Babies' Names* is the ultimate one-stop guide.

BOOKS

Perfect CV

Max Eggert

All you need to get it right first time

- Are you determined to succeed in your job search?
- Do you need guidance on how to make a great first impression?
- Do you want to make sure your CV stands out?

Bestselling *Perfect CV* is essential reading for anyone who's applying for jobs. Written by a leading HR professional with years of experience, it explains what recruiters are looking for, gives practical advice about how to show yourself in your best light, and provides real-life examples to help you improve your CV. Whether you're a graduate looking to take the first step on the career ladder, or you're planning an all-important job change, *Perfect CV* will help you stand out from the competition.

BOOKS

Perfect Psychometric Test Results

Joanna Moutafi and Ian Newcombe

All you need to get it right first time

- Have you been asked to sit a psychometric test?
- Do you want guidance on the sorts of questions you'll be asked?
- Do you want to make sure you perform to the best of your abilities?

Perfect Psychometric Test Results is the ideal guide for anyone who wants to secure their ideal job. Written by a team from Kenexa, one of the UK's leading compilers of psychometric tests, it explains how each test works, gives helpful pointers on how to get ready, and provides professionally constructed sample questions for you to try out at home. It also contains an in-depth section on online testing – the route that more and more recruiters are choosing to take. Whether you're a graduate looking to take the first step on the career ladder, or you're planning an all-important job change, *Perfect Psychometric Test Results* has everything you need to make sure you stand out from the competition.

BOOKS

Perfect Pub Quiz

David Pickering

All you need to stage a great quiz

- Who invented the cat-flap?
- Which is the largest island in the world?
- What is tofu made of?

Perfect Pub Quiz is the ideal companion for all general knowledge nuts. Whether you're organising a quiz night in your local or you simply want to get in a bit of practice on tricky subjects, *Perfect Pub Quiz* has all the questions and answers. With topics ranging from the Roman Empire to *Little Britain* and from the Ryder Cup to Alex Rider, this easy-to-use quiz book will tax your brain and provide hours of fun.

BOOKS

Order more titles in the *Perfect* series
from your local bookshop, or have them delivered
direct to your door by Bookpost.

☐ Perfect Answers to Interview Questions	Max Eggert	9781905211722	£7.99
☐ Perfect Babies' Names	Rosalind Fergusson	9781905211661	£5.99
☐ Perfect CV	Max Eggert	9781905211739	£7.99
☐ Perfect Interview	Max Eggert	9781905211746	£7.99
☐ Perfect Numerical Test Results	Joanna Moutafi and Ian Newcombe	9781905211333	£7.99
☐ Perfect Personality Profiles	Helen Baron	9781905211821	£7.99
☐ Perfect Psychometric Test Results	Joanna Moutafi and Ian Newcombe	9781905211678	£7.99
☐ Perfect Pub Quiz	David Pickering	9781905211692	£6.99
☐ Perfect Punctuation	Stephen Curtis	9781905211685	£5.99
☐ Perfect Readings for Weddings	Jonathan Law	9781905211098	£6.99
☐ Perfect Wedding Speeches and Toasts	George Davidson	9781905211777	£5.99

Free post and packing
Overseas customers allow £2 per paperback

Phone: 01624 677237

Post: Random House Books
c/o Bookpost, PO Box 29, Douglas, Isle of Man IM99 1BQ

Fax: 01624 670 923

email: bookshop@enterprise.net

Cheques (payable to Bookpost) and credit cards accepted

Prices and availability subject to change without notice.
Allow 28 days for delivery.
When placing your order, please state if you do not
wish to receive any additional information.

www.randomhouse.co.uk